# Psychology from Scripture
### Bridging the Gap

How to think more spiritually
to solve everyday problems.

**By**
**Dr. Earle H. Williams, II**
Norfolk, Virginia

*For Gerry, my brother in Christ.*

Editors
Robin Miller and Robin Wooling

Cover design
Karen Newburn

*Dr. Earle Williams*
*5/9/2016*

*Psychology from Scripture: Bridging the Gap*
*Dr. Earle H. Williams, II*

Published by:
Earle H. Williams, II, Psy.D.
P. O. Box 7611
Norfolk, VA 23509
www.drearle.com

ISBN: 978-0-9700540-0-5
LOC: 00-91337

Printed in the United States by
Morris Publishing
3212 East Highway 30
Kearney, NE 68847
1-800-650-7888

# Table of Contents

# Acknowledgments

I have so many to thank it is difficult to know where to begin. First, I would like to thank my Lord and Savior Jesus Christ and the Holy Spirit for the inspiration, guidance, and perseverance to see this work to completion. Along the way I was helped by many, not the least of whom are my deceased parents who brought me up to worship God, which has become the foundation of my life. Friends such as Dale, Major Fowler, Paul and Barbara Weinberg, and others supported this effort with their money, friendship, and love. Without my many readers like Jan W., Robin M., Robin W., Kim W., Elizabeth B. and Toureia W., this effort would have been impossible. I would also like to thank my wife for her patience and encouragement as well as my son for going with me on the road to give workshops and to sell the audio version of this book. Thank you so very, very much.

# Preface

This book is not intended to disparage the science/art of psychology nor to compromise the Bible as the Word of God. It is my belief that the incorporation of Scripture into any profession, be it engineering, finance, carpentry, plumbing, politics, science, social sciences, music, the arts, or any other field of study, can only enhance the objectives of that endeavor. For instance, did you know that Mozart and Leonardo da Vinci were extremely devout in their belief of God? Also, Albert Einstein, considered one of the most brilliant men of the 20th century, said his theories were an attempt to read the mind of God.

Society has labeled men such as Mozart and Einstein as geniuses. The common use of this term, as found in Webster's Seventh New Collegiate Dictionary, is "a person who has a strongly marked capacity, transcendent mental superiority, a person with a very high intelligence quotient." Interestingly enough, the synonym for genius is gift. In this case it is not a person. As such, genius may be less of a mark of intelligence and more of a gift. Perhaps it is one of the spiritual gifts spoken of in I Corinthians 12:7-11. It would follow, then, that invoking the spirit of God in all worthwhile professions or endeavors makes sense.

Psychologists are counselors. One of the Scriptural names ascribed to God is that of "*Wonderful Counselor*" (Isaiah 9:31). What I present in this book is how God has lifted my profession to the level of a ministry. Let me make it abundantly clear that my use of Scripture is non-denominational. From my point of view, I believe God is too big to be fully contained in any one religion. For that reason, this book is based on Scripture, which all Christian denominations have in common. Differences that separate us into various groups and factions are of minor concern. What is common about us is our belief that we are children of God, redeemed by the blood of Jesus Christ our Lord and Savior, and guided by the Holy Spirit. I also believe that the Holy Bible is the Word of God. All Scripture quoted in this text can be found in any Biblical translation.

Although this book contains examples of how Scripture can be applied in particular situations, it is not a cookbook of Biblical applications to clinical interventions. Rather, I hope to inspire you to bring your spirituality with you when you work and play. This way you can be led by the Holy Spirit to include God in your life. You do not have to be a theologian or have a formal education of the Bible to include God in every aspect of your life.

# Introduction

Welcome to *Psychology from Scripture*. Let me explain why I decided to write this book. Although I am not a theologian, I am a Christian. Like many of you, I find there is a gap between what is preached on Sunday and how people choose to behave the rest of the week. As I reflected on why there is such a gap between what we hear on Sunday and its application to our daily lives, I developed a theory.

This country was founded on the principle of religious freedom. That is why the first settlers came to America. Somehow America moved away from this founding principle and embraced the concept of separation of church and state. As a result, America has experienced a steady decline in moral values once the bedrock of this nation. In addition, we have had steady increases in crime, lost youth, and greed. While there are obvious benefits to a system where church and state are separate, such as no forced religion or religious favoritism, there are also drawbacks.

On the downside, the most troubling consideration is that religious practice becomes something separate from everyday living. Thus, this separation becomes fertile ground for ungodliness to be exhibited Monday through Saturday and for self-righteousness to surface only on Sunday. Because of this gap, we are at risk of deviant behavior. It then becomes easier to justify and support atrocities such as slavery, apartheid, criminal activity, religious persecution, child abuse, spouse abuse, and the like.

Cultures with the strongest spiritual convictions seem to be those for whom their religion and/or spirituality are an integral part of their culture. This can be seen in parts of South America, in some

African tribes, and even within cults. Their religion is infused into every aspect of their lives. Think about it. If you want to bridge the Sunday-to-weekday gap, your spirituality must take priority in your life and not remain just an appendage. As is found in James 1:22, "*Do not deceive yourselves by just listening to His Word: instead, put it into practice.*" My purpose and goal in producing this material is to help make your faith in God a living, dynamic, fulfilling experience every day.

What you are about to read is not about religion because religion is a human product. Rather, it is about Scripture and living a Christian life. As such, I am more interested in our commonalities as opposed to our religious differences, and the Bible is the one thing all Christians have in common. My purpose for writing *Psychology from Scripture* is consistent with what Paul says in Ephesians 4:22 - 23: "*You must lay aside your former way of life and the old self which deteriorates through illusion and desire, and acquire a fresh, spiritual way of thinking.*" In this book, my objective is for you to embrace a spiritual way of thinking.

Professionally, I am a licensed Clinical Psychologist. The word *psyche* is derived from a Greek word meaning soul. Technically, a psychologist is a *soul doctor*. It is, therefore, fitting that a psychologist examine the Bible and use it as a way of helping clients find the peace Jesus promised us when He said to the apostles "*I give you peace, the kind of peace that only I can give. It is not the peace that this world can give. So don't be worried or afraid,*" (John 14:27).

For about ten years, I have been integrating Scripture with psychology as I counsel clients in my private practice. One might ask why a Clinical Psychologist would concern himself with scriptural references to practice psychotherapy. The answer is very simple. As a Christian, everything I do must be consistent with God's word. In a profession such as this - where my aim is to provide a level of comfort to those in emotional distress — who better to have as a role model than the Holy Spirit? Jesus promised to send the Comforter, the Holy Spirit of God, to guide the apostles and all Christians as we traverse the road of mortal life to gain eternal life. Although we all have heard of the Holy Spirit, it seems that little is said about Him in some churches.

Let me explain part of the role of the Holy Spirit. Sometimes the Holy Spirit is called the Comforter or Helper. He is the invisible presence of God who helps us to be content in the world and to contend with the world. He reminds us that Jesus our Savior is alive. He also helps us to understand God's word. He gives us the power to do things for God that will last forever (The International Student Bible For Catholics, New Testament Edition, p. 296). I have also heard that the Holy Spirit is God's mark of ownership on us. As the Lord has lifted my profession to the level of a ministry, I, too, have become a disciple using the Holy Spirit as my role model. The combining of psychology and scripture was not a practice I sought, but rather it came as a gift.

In 1987, while working at a large state mental hospital, I met a middle-aged woman who had a history of self-mutilation. As a result of ministering to her in one session, she gained insight and peace, and I gained an amazing new understanding of human behavior. After this remarkable encounter, I asked the Lord to use me in my profession to continue to minister His Word as I counseled.

After I left the hospital to start my own business, I had another occasion to use my profession as a ministry. A woman brought her 11-year-old son to me because he had been kicked out of school. It seems he had drawn a picture of Satan, holding a hatchet, chasing the teacher. School officials were upset over this drawing, and the mother was frantic.

Obviously, graduate school had not prepared me to cope with

this, but God did. Using techniques and understandings you will find later in this chapter, we (God and I) resolved the problem. It was at this time I began using the following disclaimer to all of my clients who allowed me to use Scripture in their therapy:

"If anything I say here is of any use at all, it is from God. If it is of no use at all, it was probably my idea and something got lost in the transmission."

I offer you the same disclaimer. If what you read here makes sense and is useful, it is from the Lord. To God be the glory!

One of my more recent applications of Scripture in a clinical outpatient setting was with an 11-year-old girl. We will call her Susan. Susan was brought into therapy because of her violent behavior. She often started fights with peers and siblings. Her mother, a devout Christian, took her daughter to church every Sunday. Susan was in psychotherapy to discover the source of her anger. We found it was as a result of her father abandoning her and her family. As we worked this out, Susan continued her aggressive behaviors.

I asked Susan if she was a Christian. She said she was. I asked if she knew anything about spiritual warfare. Susan knew a little bit about it, but she did believe in God, angels, and demons. I told her that all of us would spend eternity with which ever master we had served on earth. I asked if she realized that everything we do on earth pleases someone in the spiritual realm.

"No."

"It's true. When you start trouble who do you think is pleased?"

"The Devil," Susan said.

"Whoever you please on earth will be your master for eternity. Since you will be spending eternity with your master, I suggest you choose your master well."

Soon after this session, Susan turned her life around, and we terminated treatment. You, too, can bring God into your life to resolve everyday psychological trials and tribulations.

# Spiritual Warfare

As you read this chapter on Spiritual Warfare, you will be introduced to new concepts and verbalizations. One such term is **thought insertion**. It is found in the <u>Diagnostic and Statistical Manual of Mental Disorders-IV</u> and is defined as *a symptom of psychosis such as Schizophrenia*. It is a patient's belief that objects such as a radio or a television can put thoughts into his head or speak to him specifically. However, my use of this term is spiritual. For purposes here, thought insertion means that not every thought that comes into your head is necessarily your own.

This concept came to me as I was treating a drug addict. Frank had used crack cocaine for over 5 years. Generally, I do not treat drug addicts because they tend to be unreliable and irresponsible. However, because his mother attended my church, I consented to work with him. We met, did an intake evaluation, and devised a treatment plan.

Treatment went well for Frank. He had his minor relapses but came back to make even more progress. Then he had a particularly intense relapse involving drugs and sexual activity that cost him his savings of about $3,000. Treatment continued. One night, prior to one of our sessions, I received what I will call a message. It wasn't a voice but more like a thought or an insight. This had never happened to me before. The message was, "If you go on a drug and sex binge again, Satan is going to take you out." The next day, during our therapy session, I shared the message with Frank. He took it seriously and worked hard to stay clean.

Frank continued to be bombarded with thoughts of drug abuse. These thoughts or impulses would occur at the strangest times.

Frank would be doing something not at all related to any drug use, and a drug thought would come. He could be washing dishes, taking out the trash, or sleeping and a thought would arise. It occurred to me that all of us have had reprehensible thoughts at sometime in our lives, thoughts so evil/repulsive we never tell anyone about them. I remind you that not all thoughts that come into our heads are ours. Some thoughts come from God, some from ourselves, and others are from demons. Here, you will learn about the sources of these types of thoughts and what you can do about them. Frank used these techniques and is a recovering drug addict.

Let me give you two more examples of how psychology found in Scripture can help you gain peace of mind. I am often called to treat people suffering from depression. Psychologists sometimes use a behavioral technique called *cognitive restructuring* or **self-talk**. Here, the therapist examines what clients may be saying to themselves that may unwittingly facilitate their own depression or poor self-esteem. When the therapist finds negative self-talk, he will instruct the client to replace it with positive self-talk. This is not a new technique or one invented by psychologists. Paul used this very same principle, as is found in Philippians 4:8: *"In conclusion, my brothers, fill your minds with those things that are good and that deserve praise; things that are true, noble, right, pure, lovely, and honorable."* So it is important to replace self-destructive thoughts with more positive thoughts, as Paul describes. Paul's words are a good defense against depression. It is also useful to focus on the peace Christ promised us. God never breaks His promise. This is similar to the psychological technique of self-talk where destructive thoughts of an individual are identified and replaced with positive and uplifting self-talk.

Another Scriptural principle I use in psychotherapy to help resolve grief and depression is forgiveness. In my opinion, forgiveness and love are the cornerstones of Christ's teachings. The way I understand it, Christ was not looking forward to His crucifixion. When He prayed to His Father in the Garden of Gethsemane, Christ asked that the cup pass from Him, but then said "*Not my will but your will be done*" (Luke 22:42). It seems to me that if Christ had died in angry resistance, His death might not have earned salvation for us. The only way Christ could die without having a negative attitude was to forgive those who crucified Him: "*Father forgive them for they know not what they do*" (Luke 23:34). This is an important lesson for us. Because the human nature of Jesus may not have been able to handle the anger engendered by the Romans crucifying Him, He took it to His Father. When a loved one dies, we may have to forgive that person for what we may feel and experience as desertion. We may even be angry with God for taking our loved one. A more common event is found in domestic disagreements. We must learn to forgive one another, whether or not there is an apology. In any instance where we feel we have been wronged, part of our healing process must involve forgiveness. Scripture commands us to love our enemies. God cannot forgive us if we are unwilling to forgive others. When Jesus taught us to pray, part of that prayer was, "*Forgive us our trespasses as we forgive others*," (Matthew 6:12, Luke 11:4).

In my studies as a psychologist, it was said that Sigmund Freud, known as the father of psychology and psychiatry, claimed that man was basically destructive. Although many mental health professionals dismiss Freud as a victim of the Victorian Age, I believe he was correct in his findings regarding the nature of man. As I reflect on my experiences both in life and as a professional, I have to agree with Freud. I believe that, left to our own desires, greed and hedonism would prevail and many would destroy themselves, their neighbors, and ultimately the world.

During the Lenten season of 1995, I made a vow to read every word of the New Testament. In it, I discovered Freud's ideas had Scriptural validity. Consider Freud's psychodynamic theories concerning the Id (what we feel is what the body wants immediately), the Ego (what we think and how we navigate reality) and the Superego (our sense of right and wrong, our morals and values or conscience) and the following scriptures:

> "But a person is tempted when he is drawn away and trapped by his own evil desire. Then his evil desire conceives and gives birth to sin; and sin, when it is full grown, gives birth to death." (James 1:14-15)

> "... lived according to our natural desires doing whatever suited the wishes of our own bodies and minds." (Ephesians 2:3)

> "They are going to end up in hell, because their God is their bodily desires." (Philippians 3:19)

If you still doubt what Freud said about human nature, consider this indictment of human nature found in Galatians 5:19-21:

> What human nature does is quite plain. It shows itself in immoral, filthy, and indecent actions, in worship of idols and witchcraft. People become enemies and they fight; they become jealous, angry, and ambitious. They separate into parties and groups; they are envious, get drunk, have orgies, and do other things like these. I warn you now as I have before; those who do these things will not possess the Kingdom of God.

These revelations found in Scripture allow me the opportunity to blend my Christianity with my profession as a psychologist, giving me direction and focus. What I treat are human desires, frailties, and weaknesses. A psychologist treats the mind so that the mind will control human nature. However, if all of human nature is so thoroughly corrupt, what real victory is there in being human? There must be more to life than being human. There must be something better, purer, and more wholesome than being human. If not, why bother treating people? Why try to ease their pain if pain is all there is? The answer to this question is found in the same chapter of Galatians that describes the problem (Galatians 5:16).

> *What I say is this; let the Spirit direct your lives, and you will not satisfy the desires of the human nature. For what our human nature wants is opposed to what the Spirit wants, and what the Spirit wants is opposed to what our human nature wants. These two are enemies, and this means that you cannot do what you want to do. If the Spirit leads you, then you are not subject to the Law* (Galatians 5:18).

This then defines my purpose for practicing psychotherapy with Christians. My job is not to cure, not just to bring their wishes and human nature under the control of their minds, but to go to the next step. My job is to clear the emotional human garbage that interferes with the Spirit. I direct my clients' minds into the light, so they will come under the control of the Holy Spirit. "*I will ask the Father, and He will give you another Helper, who will stay with you forever. He is the Spirit, who will reveal the truth about God*" (John 14:16-17). Psychology from Scripture is a description of how this is done and the various Scriptures I use in psychotherapy.

Another important point in my analysis of the Bible is the distinction between burdens of demons and the burdens of God. After all, we as Christians know that as followers of Christ, we glorify in tribulations (James 1:12). All of Christ's apostles suffered, and we will also. Consider what Peter writes, "*Be glad about this, even though it may be necessary for you to be sad for a while because of the many kinds of trials you suffer. Their purpose is to prove that your faith is genuine*" (Peter 1:6-7). There are many other reasons why we, as children of God, are admonished. One such reason is found in Hebrews 12: 5-8: "*Have you forgotten the encouraging words which God speaks to you his sons? My sons, pay attention when the Lord corrects you, and do not be discouraged when he rebukes you. Because the Lord corrects everyone he loves, and disciplines everyone he accepts as a son. Endure what you suffer as being a father's admonishment; your suffering shows that God is treating you as his sons."* Yet, not all burdens are from God. It is crucial to understand the difference between the Lord's burdens and those of Satan.

Lest anyone misunderstand, I am not proposing that the Scripture is a panacea. It is not. You cannot just expose everyone to the truth of the Lord and think everything is going to be OK. Everyone is not going to embrace the truth. Even in Jesus' time, not everyone believed. One of His own betrayed Him. Even those who believed had problems with Jesus' resurrection such as Thomas, His apostle. Even Peter, upon whom He built His church, was subject to violent passion and denial. The light of God, His patience and grace is only for His children, and we have to know how to access it. Only by accepting Jesus as Lord and Savior can we be saved. Be warned we are not all children of God. Many are under the influence of their father, Satan. Others may just be free spirits. In my role of psychologist, I have worked with all types of people. As a Clinical Psychologist, I teach people how to gain mental control over human nature; however, the optimal mental state is to have the mind under the control of the Holy Spirit.

## The Mind

Clinical Psychology deals with the mind. Scripture delineates three major parts of the body that bring an individual in harmony with the will of God. They are ears to hear, the mind, and the heart. We do not comprehend God's Word if our minds are dull. When seeds of God's Word are spread on rocky soil, the devil takes the Word out of our minds. Paul teaches us to be of a single mind. When depression comes, he teaches us to think on things that are pure and of good report. The mind is mentioned several times in Scripture. In many Baptist churches, Christians often thank God for waking up in their right minds. This is related to Scripture describing a man's deliverance from demons which left him *"clothed and in his right mind"* (Luke 8:35). Paul describes three specific states of mind in Philippians:

1. **The single mind:** we should all have the common purpose of fighting together for the faith and gospel.

2. **The spiritual mind:** we should share love, not be selfish, and be humble.

3. **The secure mind:** we should stand fast in the Lord (4:1), and we will receive the peace of God (4:7)

The profound relationship between the mind and the will of God that is mediated by the Spirit is also found in Scripture. *"Be ye transformed by the renewing of your mind, that ye may prove what is the good, and acceptable, and the perfect will of God"* (Romans 12:1&2). The mind plays a crucial part in loving God. We are commanded to love God with all our heart and our mind (Matthew 22:37).

Psychologists are the only doctoral level professionals who deal exclusively with the mind and how it functions. My job as a Christian psychologist is not to heal as much as it is to undo mental knots, so that the power of God can flow through my clients, healing their minds. My analogy comes from my 20 years as a plumber prior to becoming a psychologist. As a psychologist I unstop the pipes carrying God's grace.

Clearly there is an intimate connection between the Word and the mind. Spirituality is facilitated by a strong mind. Emotional garbage such as childhood trauma, rape, abuse, hate, lust, etc. can twist the mind into knots. Some knots are double and triple knots. Others are very old knots formed during childhood. When emotional knots are undone, healing begins.

As Christians, we are all targets in spiritual warfare. It is therefore incumbent on us to know how demons try to defeat us. In any type of battle, we must have a plan. We cannot have a plan if we do not know the enemy's strengths and weaknesses. On our own, all we can do is resist demons; but knowing what weapons we have at our disposal and knowing the tactics of Satan, we are able to put on the whole armor of God which allows us to surpass our mortal resistance.

We must know exactly who we are in order to fight a good fight. When we know who we are, we understand the meaning of "*We fight not against flesh and blood...*" (Ephesians 6:12).

## Identity

The acquisition of identity is crucial in the process of human development. It is identity which sets the stage for all human accomplishments, sense of worth/self-esteem, career choice, partner choices, and many other major life choices. That is, we choose our career, life-style, and mates in a way that is consistent with our own sense of identity. If our sense of identity is flawed, we are at risk of making incorrect choices.

Whatever we choose as our primary identity usually becomes the driving force of our existence. Consider a person whose main identity is that of a man. At the very least, he is at risk of becoming macho. A person whose primary identity is that of a woman could possibly become a feminist. The list of various possible identities goes on and on. Although these identities are not good or bad in and of themselves, the point is that they can become our driving motivational force for existence and can lead us into areas such as careers or mates not chosen for us and away from God's will for our life.

Erik Erikson, a famous psychologist who trained under Sigmund Freud, did extensive research in the area of psychosocial development. His theory was a radical departure from Freud, his mentor. Freud's theories of psychosexual development held that, among other things, man is inherently destructive and that our entire personality is shaped by early childhood experiences, especially the mother/child relationship. Erikson believed that personality was shaped not only by genetics and the mother/child relationship but also to a greater degree by our environment. As such, he developed a list of psychosocial stages of development, which occur at specific age ranges. Erikson's stages of development are:

| STAGE | AGE |
|---|---|
| Trust vs. Mistrust | Birth - 1 |
| Autonomy vs. Shame & Doubt | 2 - 4 |
| Initiative vs. Guilt | 4 - 5 |
| Industry vs. Inferiority | 6 - 11 |
| **Identity Repudiation vs. Identity Diffusion** | **12 - 18** |
| Intimacy & Solidarity vs. Isolation | Young Adulthood |
| Generativity vs. Self Absorption/Stagnation | Middle Years |
| Integrity vs. Despair | Old Age |

As you can see, identity is a crucial developmental task of psychosocial development that occurs in the middle of the developmental cycle. It is a task of adolescence to define identity, and some people never manage to resolve this issue, even into adulthood. Childhood upbringing, emotional and physical environment, race, gender, spirituality, and other factors can either facilitate or hinder successful resolution of any stage of development.

In Erikson's case, the issue of identity was especially important because he did not know his father. As such, he was left to parent himself. To symbolize this concern, he gave himself the surname of Erikson, as he was his own son. Instead of having a father to identify with, he identified with himself.

## Identity and Spirituality

Jesus identified with His father, God. Satan's first two challenges when he tempted Jesus in the desert dealt with identity. *"If you are the Son of God, command that these stones become loaves of bread...If you are the Son of God, throw yourself down"* (Matthew 4:3-6). However, in striking contrast to Erikson, Jesus knew His father intimately.

Because the concept of identity is of crucial importance to our spiritual and psychological well being, we need to be abundantly sure of who we are. Interestingly enough, when Jesus would not prove to Satan that He was the Son of God, Satan tried to give Jesus a human identity by appealing to His flesh, by telling Jesus to turn the stones to bread. It was only then that Jesus, in response to Satan's temptation affirmed His identity by telling him, *"You shall not put the Lord, your God, to the test."*

I put it to you that one's identity should be that which is the most important and enduring characteristic to that individual. For if being a human is your most important characteristic, you are at risk of becoming hedonistic (a pleasure seeker) and most concerned with earthly pleasure. Instead of identifying yourself as a human being with a spiritual side, I assert that you are a spiritual being with a temporary and fragile human side. That which is spiritual about us is most likely the part of us which God made in His image and likeness. It is in all likelihood that our spirits are the part of us that will endure after our bodies are laid to rest. It is that part which we refer to as "going home" at funerals. Perhaps this is why we are instructed to *"Seek ye first the kingdom of heaven"* (Matthew 6:33).

That we are spiritual beings with human experiences justifies Christ's admonishment, *"What does it profit a man to gain the whole world and suffer the loss of his soul?"* (Mark 9:36-38). You are not a human being with a spiritual side. You are a spiritual being with a temporary human side.

## Why Be Concerned with Spiritual Warfare?

In this modern age of miracle drugs, New Age religions, computers connected to the Internet, powerful cars, and rockets to outer space, why should we be interested in or concerned with such an ancient concept as spiritual warfare? The most compelling reason is because it does exist, and all of our modern conveyances cannot fight its power. Spiritual warfare is like gravity; you do not have to believe it to be affected by it. Spiritual warfare, like gravity, is always at work. I assure you that if you jump up in the air, you will come back down. You do not have to believe that the world is round, but if you travel far enough in the same direction, you will return to where you started. So, if you accept the reality of spiritual warfare, you may ask what does it have to do with the loss of joy, depression, insanity, and many other afflictions. Mostly, it is because there are many physical and spiritual things demons can do. These things not only affect our chances of gaining eternal life, but they can also make life on earth a living hell.

Catholic theologians tell me that the story of Job is a metaphor or a story made up to teach a lesson. Perhaps there never was a person named Job, but as part of the inspired Word of God, we can learn much by analyzing it. In the book of Job, God admonished Satan not to kill Job (Job 1:12). This suggests at least two things: 1) Satan is not stronger than God and 2) Satan can literally kill you just as he did Job's children, and he can take all of your wealth or inflict you with debilitating diseases, just as he did Job.

Here is a list of things demons do, as written in the New Testament:
1. Cause the inability to talk (Matthew 9:32-33 & Luke 11:14)
2. Cause insanity (Matthew 5:1-3 & Luke 8:35-36)
3. Cause general trouble (Luke 6:18)
4. Cause promiscuity (Luke 8:2)
5. Cause the Word to be taken out of our minds (Luke 8:11-12)
6. Cause one to be bent over, i.e. arthritis (Luke 13:10-13)
7. Cause murder (John 7:20 & 8:44)
8. Take control (Acts 5:3 & 10:37)
9. Cause paralysis & lameness (Acts 8:7)
10. Give power to predict the future (Acts 16:16-20)
11. Cause diseases (Acts 19:12)

## Spiritual Warfare

I began combining psychology and scripture over 10 years ago while working at a large state hospital in Virginia. I met a female patient who had been in and out of the hospital for over 10 years. She was suffering from a psychosis that compelled her to slash her arms. On both arms, from her wrists to her elbows, were masses of scars where she had been mutilating herself. She was caught up in a cycle in which she would be admitted to the hospital where she was stabilized on psychotropic medications for about two months and sent back out to the community. After a month or so, she would start having visions and hallucinating, and start slashing her arms again. She would be readmitted to the hospital and the cycle would continue.

Although this woman was not assigned to me, one day I asked her to come into my office. This was the second time I had seen her and I knew of her condition. I asked her, "Why do you slash your wrists?" To her surprise (and mine) no one had ever asked her this question before. Prior to this, I had asked various psychiatrists who administered the woman's psychotropic drugs what the origins of visions and hallucinations were, but they couldn't give me a satisfactory answer.

The woman went on to tell me that she had visions of Moses in which he would ask her for blood. I thought about this for a moment and said to her, "What if the man you see in your visions is really a demon disguised as Moses?" This gave her cause for concern. In all likelihood, it probably shook the very foundations of her demonic visions. I went on to say, "Don't you think that the death of Jesus Christ on the cross ended blood sacrifices?" She agreed that it had. Finally, after about an hour or so, I was able to convince her that her visions were probably caused by demons disguised as Moses. We only had one session. Soon afterwards, she was discharged back into the community. I never saw this woman again in my remaining two-and-a-half years at that hospital. I don't know if she was cured, but I think that she was certainly helped.

This marked the changeover of my profession into a ministry. After this episode, I did a relapse prevention group therapy with schizophrenics, based on the book of Proverbs. I called my group "Psychology of the Bible." It was a hit. My patients loved it and learned a great deal from it, as did I. In our meetings, we would take turns reading and explaining verses from the book of Proverbs. We learned about how to choose a mate, how to choose friends, good advice, wisdom, making plans, and other pragmatic lessons necessary for living a good life. I chose Proverbs because I felt it was the most comprehensive book of Scripture dealing with how a person should live. I hoped this would encourage them to act responsibly when discharged back into the community. After facilitating this group for about 6 months, I was transferred to another building. To my regret, I didn't have an occasion to use Scripture directly in my practice for another couple of years.

Everyone has problems. To effectively deal with these problems, we must address the physical, emotional, and spiritual aspects of our issues. The most important and the most often neglected aspect of an individual's being (and most often neglected in psychotherapy, in this doctor's opinion) is the spiritual side. Conversely, those that deal with the spiritual often neglect the physical and emotional aspects. Mental illness is a very real phenomenon and cannot be dismissed solely with prayer. We live in a world where we think we can separate the physical from the emotional and/or both from the spiritual. As a psychologist, I know that the body-mind separation is artificial. The reason for this separation is for convenience. Because no man can fully understand all realms of human experience, we separate them into categories so different individuals can be specialists at specific aspects of functioning.

Many problems have their origin in the harboring of negative emotions. Of all the negative emotions that we can have, possibly the most dangerous one is hate and all its derivatives. I have concluded that hate, anger, and so forth, are the most powerful demons because Jesus Christ agreed that the most powerful virtue is love. Love is the hallmark of the two most important commandments (Matthew 22:36-40). Conversely, hate and anger must be the most dangerous of all emotions and the most powerful demons. Anger is the negative emotion mentioned in the Bible more frequently than any other. Parents are admonished not to *provoke their children to wrath* (Ephesians 6:4). All of us are warned not to *let the sun set on our anger nor give place to the Devil* (Ephesians 4:26-27). Socially, anger and hate are the principal emotions causing the most horrific crimes against self and humanity. Anger is the root cause of many human problems such as war, murder, torture, slavery, ethnic cleansing, adultery, and rape. Psychologically, emotions of hate and anger are at the root of many mental illnesses. Considering negative emotions from this point of view suggests that functions of the mind affect behavior and vice versa. If this is true, then the best way to resolve emotional problems may be to deal with them as both a psychological and a spiritual issue.

As a clinical psychologist, I find that I am in contact with Christians and others who feel spiritually defeated. Most do not know that we are all engaged in spiritual warfare. Of the minority of those who realize this, even fewer know how to fight against it. Some confuse spiritual warfare with physical warfare. Clients come to therapy with questions like, "Why me? It's so unfair," "He or she has it in for me," "Mine is a racial issue, or a gender issue," etc. Often people are surprised and taken aback when I respond with my question, "Why not you?" After the initial shock wears off, I will ask other questions such as, "Are you a Christian? Do you believe in God? Do you believe the Bible to be the Word of God? Is Jesus Christ God?" If the answers are affirmative, this then becomes the foundation of our therapy as we use psycho-spiritual healing to resolve not only the clients' problems, but also their attitude towards them.

I've had a number of people come to me with complaints of sexual or racial harassment suffered on the job. These people absorb the hate and anger put upon them by others to such an extent that they are plagued with nightmares, nervousness, stress, tension, and depression. One of the ways that I help them cope is to help them understand that they are not fighting a physical or worldly battle; rather their fight is against spiritual forces (Ephesians 6:10-13). This gives them the opportunity to fight the problem not just on a physical level but on the spiritual level as well. I certainly would not suggest to anyone not to file charges against the perpetrators of harassment. Rather, if they fight this battle on the spiritual level, spiritual self-defense can give them some peace of mind (John 14:27) so they don't have to experience the negative symptoms that they had previously. But before we deal with spiritual self-defense, we need to deal with the aspects of the spiritual realm.

## The Spiritual Realm

What does the spiritual realm have to do with Christians in particular and people in general? What we need to know about spiritual warfare is summed up in Paul's writing found in Ephesians 6:14-18. This gives us a better idea of just what it is we are battling. Paul says we *"fight not against flesh and blood but against principalities and powers in high places."* This suggests that people are not our problem. This might be why Jesus Christ, when he was on the cross, was able to say *"Father, forgive them for they know not what they do"* (Luke 23:34). Jesus knew that those responsible for His death and suffering were working both according to the will of His Father and through Satan.

However, many of them knew exactly what they were doing. Consider the example of Pontius Pilate. Now surely Pontius Pilate knew what he was doing in condemning an innocent man, and he had wanted to set Him free (Luke 23:20). Pilate's wife even told her husband to have nothing to do with the man (Matthew 27:19). Pilate chose to please Christ's accusers. He condemned Jesus to death (Luke 33:1-25). Surely the chief priests and teachers of the law knew Jesus was a good man (Matthew 21:15, Mark 6:2-6, and Luke 6: 11 & 20-26). After all, they had seen his miracles; they had heard his preaching; and Jesus Christ had told them that he had come to fulfill the Old Testament prophecies and fulfill the law. Still, they couldn't accept that He was the Messiah and saw Him as a blasphemer (John 9:13-18). So, how was it that Christ was able to say in all honesty, *"Father, forgive them for they know not what they do"* (Luke 23:34)? Jesus knew it was Satan's work. Yet, it was also God's plan and Jesus knew his purpose was to die for men's sins. He retained the power over His life, not Satan.

This brings us to the issue of spiritual warfare. As noted earlier, spiritual warfare is like gravity. You do not have to believe in the existence of gravity to be affected by it. Spiritual warfare is much the same way. All of us, whether we know it or not, like it or not, accept it or not, are affected by what transpires in the spiritual realm. Spiritual warfare is based on the concept that there are entities on a spiritual level - in a spiritual realm - that are invested either in our success or our destruction. I contend that these forces can be divided into two basic categories: forces for good and forces for evil. Forces for evil hope that you do not believe in their existence. This gives them the element of surprise. The Bible calls the forces of evil: Satan, demons, angels of darkness, and evil spirits. The forces of good are referred to as God, Jesus, the Holy Spirit, and angels (Seraphim, Cherubim, etc.).

Pat Robertson gives a very concise and good view of the spiritual realm in one of his pamphlets entitled "Anger, Demons and End-times." In this pamphlet, he describes the nature of angels, de-

mons, Satan's power and ultimate destiny, and demon posses-
sion. He also deals with whether or not a Christian can be
possessed and with exorcism. I would like to share with you what
he says about angels:

> *Angels are spiritual beings created by God to serve Him. They are very*
> *powerful beings who function as God's messengers. In numerous in-*
> *stances in the Bible, angels appeared to people claiming they had come*
> *as messengers from God. The New Testament tells us they are also*
> *ministering spirits, sent to look after human beings who are their heirs*
> *(Hebrews 1:14).*

Jesus seemed to indicate that little children have angels assigned
to them, for he said, *"Their angels always behold the face of God,"* (Matthew 18:10).

The concept of guardian angels has its basis in the Bible. In
addition to worker angels (who deliver God's messages and look
out for humans), there are archangels, and angel princes such as
Michael, described in chapter nine of the Book of Jude. Scripture
seems to indicate that he represents an entire nation (Daniel
10:13). Although we do not know what angels look like, the Bible
mentions some angelic features. In the first chapter of Ezekiel, it
tells of a vision in which the prophet saw *"four living creatures in*
*human form"* who were so holy that they appeared as flames of
fire. These creatures seemed to be like men, yet they had four
wings and multiple faces (Ezekiel 1:5-6). They responded instantly
to God's spirit. Another mention of angels occurs in the Book of
Isaiah where angels called Seraphim have six wings (Isaiah 6:2,6).
Another groups of angels are called Cherubim. Seemingly, Cherubim were present to cover the very holiness of God Himself, and
on the lid of the Ark of the Covenant, their wings formed the
mercy seat for the presence of the Lord (Exodus 23:18-22). Angels
are magnificent creatures, not at all the tiny, childlike cherubs that
we see in Renaissance art. Their power is so great that just one

angel was able to destroy 185,000 Assyrian soldiers in one night (II Kings 19:35). Their presence is so awesome that those who see them have been known to fall unconscious on the ground or to voluntarily prostrate themselves (Daniel 10:9). Angelic power was also recorded in the time of Passover when the angel of death slew every first-born male Egyptian.

Now that we have an idea of the nature of angels, what then is a demon? A demon can be defined as a fallen angel. When Satan, who was the very highest angel (Lucifer), rebelled against God, he took a large number of angels with him in rebellion. When this rebellion failed, Satan and his hosts were cast out of heaven. These former angels are now known as demons (Isaiah 14:12-15; Ezekiel 28:12-19; Luke 10:18; Revelation 12:3-9; Matthew 12:43-45, 25:41; II Peter 2:4; Ephesians 6:12; Jude 6). In the same way that angels can reach the very height of spirituality, demons have the ability to reach down into great depths of hatred, bitterness, and perversion. Demons seem to be interested in tormenting people, possessing them and leading them away from God and His truth. Just as the angels have archangels and higher powers, the demons have what are called principalities and powers. There is conflict in the invisible world between God's loyal messengers and demonic hosts. Knowledge of your enemy is vital to engaging in any kind of warfare.

In warfare, you need to know as much as you can about your enemy in order to have a reasonable expectation of winning the battle. However, you also need to know about your allies. To be an effective spiritual warrior, you have to understand the nature of warfare, some of the tactics used by the enemy, and what your responses can be to fight back. Examples of spiritual warfare will help us understand more about this. Jesus is the supreme spiritual warrior and our best role model. For example, when Jesus was telling His apostles about how He was going to be tortured, and finally crucified, Peter reacted to Jesus' words by pulling out his sword and saying that he would not let anyone hurt his Master. Jesus did not personally admonish Peter, by name, but replied, "*Get away from me Satan! You are an obstacle in my way, because these thoughts of yours don't come from God but from man*" (Matthew 16:22-23). Jesus knew that Peter was not the problem, but rather it was Satan working through Peter. This is consistent with why God the Father declares, "*Never take revenge, my friends, but instead let God's anger do it. For the Scripture says, "I will take revenge, I will pay back, says the Lord*" (Romans 12:19-20). As our father, God knows that we don't handle anger very well. This is not to say that we do not have the right to vengeance or anger, but just that we have problems resolving anger properly. God the Father, in His almighty mercy and omnipotence, took from us the responsibility of looking for vengeance.

Another reference in the Bible tells us why God took the responsibility of vengeance from us where it says, "*Do not let the sun set on your anger, nor give place to the Devil*" (Ephesians 4:26-27). In other words, when we get angry and allow negative feelings to fester within us, the demons are permitted to work through us and in us. When we looked at Job, we learned that Satan and demons needed permission to inhabit or torment. Job was a good and upright man, and Satan had no point of entry into him. This is why Satan had to get permission from God to torment him. In the same way, leaving anger inside of us to fester, we open the door, giving demons permission to torment us. With that in mind, let's examine the demonic tactics common in spiritual warfare.

## Demonic Tactics in Spiritual Warfare

Demons have a variety of weapons at their disposal with which to carry out their jobs. One such weapon is that of *thought insertion* (John 13:2). This concept is based on the premise that not all thoughts that come into the mind are necessarily yours. All of us, at one time or another, have had ugly thoughts. We have had thoughts that are so disgusting that it is likely we have never ever confided in anybody else about them. Many of us are plagued with these types of thoughts on a regular basis. Most of us get brief flashes of disgusting and vile thoughts that come into our minds. Well, I have good news for you. There is a psychological technique very effective in dispelling ruminations and intrusive thoughts. It is called *thought stopping* and it is very simple. Wear an elastic band on your wrist. Every time the thought comes into your head, snap the band on the inner wrist. This will sting momentarily but will immediately stop the thought. It will then be necessary to replace that ugly thought with a positive one. Do this enough times and the ugly thoughts will no longer return. This technique can be combined with spirituality.

These vile intrusions you experienced were not necessarily your thoughts. Some thoughts that come into your mind may have been placed there. These thoughts can be either negative or positive. It is a fact that thoughts can originate from God, demons, or self. In this discussion, we will focus on the latter two types of thoughts. The good news about this is that we do not have to claim ownership of negative thoughts. It has been my experience that demonic thoughts are usually those that are negative and, generally speaking, totally unrelated to what an individual is doing or thinking at the time that the thought comes. Godly and positive thoughts are generally consistent with what we are thinking and doing at the time and are always pure.

In order to understand this concept, we have to remember that angels, regardless of whether they belong to God or Satan, are incapable of reading your mind. Only God knows your heart and your mind. This is why demonic thoughts will not be consistent with what you are thinking. For instance, let's say a substance abuser, who has been clean for six months with no thought of drugs in his head, is sitting and watching television, minding his own business, apparently successful in kicking the habit. All of a sudden, the thought of drugs pops into his mind. Now, this is not necessarily his thought, but rather it is a tactic that the demons use to influence a person's behavior. Such unwanted thoughts need to be resisted, repelled and rejected as foreign. We can be attacked with thoughts of lust, thoughts of greed, thoughts of theft, thoughts of anger, etc. We can be walking in a store and see something we like, and all of a sudden put it in our pockets. We may not even have been thinking about stealing anything, but the thought just comes into our heads and we act on impulse. Although this is less likely to happen to an adult, it is extremely common with impulsive youth. Understanding that not all thoughts in your head are necessarily yours helps you to recognize these kinds of thoughts and gives you the right to reject and resist them.

On the other hand, we can have positive thoughts that are from God. Only God can read our hearts and our minds. Only the Holy Spirit dwelling in us can know the things that we are thinking. For instance, while you are sitting in church, the collection plate comes to you. As you reach for your customary five dollars to put in the plate, you have a second thought. You have just received your income tax return of one thousand dollars and have a thought to give God His 10%, so instead you write a check for a hundred dollars. This is a thought from God. I call this weapon of warfare *thought insertion*.

Another weapon of spiritual warfare is *temptation*. This is exemplified by the temptations of Christ by Satan when He was in the desert. As we look at the temptations of Christ, we find that they consisted of playing on human desires of hunger, fear, power, and identity. *"If you are the Son of God, command that these stones be made bread." "If thou be the Son of God cast thyself down." "All these things will I give thee if thou wilt fall down and worship me,"* (Matthew 4:1-10). We find that temptation is common to man (I Corinthians 10:13 and James 1:14-15). We know that God is always with us and is always in control of the intensity of the temptation. That is, God will not allow us to be tempted beyond our ability to endure (1 Corinthians 10:13). Just as with Job, Satan first received permission from God to tempt him. God gave Satan a limit and said, "*You cannot kill him*" (Job 1:12). This shows that God will limit our temptations and torment not to exceed His limit for us. Additionally, Jesus experienced all of the temptations with which we struggle: desires of the flesh, desires of the mind, questioning one's identity, and so forth. All of these temptations have been conquered for us by Jesus (Hebrews 4:15). Even though temptation is common to man, God is not the source of temptation, but the giver of wisdom and strength to overcome. Additionally, we will be rewarded for overcoming temptation (James 1:12-18). God will give us a way out of temptation as Jesus said He would when He taught us to pray, "*Deliver us from evil*" (Matthew 6:9-13, 1 Corinthians 10:13, and Luke 11:2-4). It is up to us to look for the escape hatch, trap door, back door, or the window, or have the legs to run. Escape is there; if "you have eyes to see or ears to hear," you will find it. There is no acceptable excuse like "I couldn't help it." Also prayer is essential in overcoming the enemy in our weakness. The Bible tells us "*In our weakness, He is strong. Resist the Devil and he will flee,*" (James 4:7). God will never give us more than we can bear without providing a way of escape. This is what Joseph had to do when propositioned by his master's wife. Even though he was innocent, he was put in prison where the Lord continued to bless him (Genesis 39:7-23). "*Every test that you have experienced is the kind that normally comes to people. But God keeps His promise, and He will not allow you to be tested beyond your power to remain firm, at the time you are put to the test, He will give you strength to endure it, and so provide you with a way out,*" (1 Corinthians 10:13).

Another weapon of demons is *burdens* placed on us. We know from scripture that God can place a burden on us when He said, "*Take my yoke and put it on you, and learn from me, because I am gentle and humble in spirit; and you will find rest. For the yoke I will give you is easy, and the load I will put on you is light*" (Matthew 11:30). Certainly we know, as Jesus Christ has taught us, if we are to be His disciples, we have to pick up our cross and follow Him (Mark 8:34). I contend that if you are not tempted or do not experience trials and tribulations, your Christianity is either weak or nonexistent. All of us who are Christians are a threat to the demonic community and are targets of Satan's wrath. We are all targets of trials and tribulations for Jesus. We will, therefore, have tribulations that have the capacity to strengthen us. What the Devil meant for evil, God can change for good. Demons use a variation of God's burden and place their own burdens on us. We need to look at some of the basic differences in these burdens to understand which is which. For me, a burden placed on me by God will never interfere with my ability to pray and worship God. However, a burden placed on you by demons will not only interfere with your ability to pray, but it will also cause you to feel helpless, hopeless, and to its extreme, to feel suicidal or homicidal. This is another weapon in our spiritual artillery. If someone you know is experiencing some sort of depression, and you find the individual is isolating himself, not going to church, and feeling helpless and hopeless, you might consider using some type of spiritual intervention along with a psychological one. "*For the sadness that is used by God brings a change of heart that leads to salvation - and there is no regret in that! But sadness that is merely human causes death,*" (2 Corinthians 7:10).

Another major demonic tactic is what I call *mind sweep.* "*The Devil comes and takes the message away from their hearts in order to keep them from believing and being saved,*" (Luke 8:12). By this I am referring to the seemingly demonic ability to wipe thoughts out of a person's mind. This is apparent when we forget to use our spiritual defenses such as resisting negative urges, praying, forgiveness, rebuking, etc., in a time of crisis. In times such as this, we are caught off guard. Perhaps this is why it is a blessing to be slow to anger and "*Happy is the person who remains faithful under trials,*" (James 1:12). Why? Because this gives us time to think before we react. This is why parents are taught not to discipline their children while they are angry. There is a psycho physiological phenomenon called the "fight or flight syndrome."

Here, it is found that when a person is afraid or angry, blood flow in the body is redirected from non-essential organs for survival to essential organs and muscles needed for fight or flight. As such, blood normally flowing to the stomach, kidney, or brain is diverted to the eyes, ears, arms, legs, etc. to prepare us for an immediate response. Additionally, our heartbeat speeds up to send even more blood to energize our essential organs and muscles. This is why when angry, we do not think very clearly.

A Biblical example of *mind sweep* can be found with Peter who disbelieved it when Jesus told him that he would deny the Lord three times before the cock crowed. Although forewarned, Peter forgot what Jesus said until the cock crowed, and he remembered what Jesus said and wept bitterly (Luke 22:54-62). Jesus had told Peter that Satan had permission to tempt him and that he would pray for him. "*Simon, Simon! Listen Satan has received permission to test all of you, to separate the good from the bad, as a farmer separates wheat from chaff*" (Luke 22:31). We can take this to mean that Satan wanted to torment Peter in some way. In all fairness, Peter was probably under intense spiritual attack, involving *mind sweep* and *fear,* another favorite demonic strategy. However, God the Father told us to "*Fear no evil,*" (Psalm 23:4).

In church, I have heard about another demonic tactic, *isolation.* That is, when one is about to be burdened by demons, often they will isolate a person. For instance, if a demon is going to place a burden of depression, despair, or temptation on us, he will wait until we are alone. He does this because he knows that we are weakest and most vulnerable when alone and/or spiritually disconnected. He tries to take all of our security away like he did with Job. If money happens to be our crutch, then he may cause us to be broke. Look at how Satan tempted Jesus with money and earthly power. "*I will give you all this power and all this wealth,*" the Devil told Him. "*It has all been given over to me, and I can give it to anyone I choose,*" (Luke 4:6). Satan tempted Jesus when he was alone and weak after 40 days and 40 nights of fasting. Jesus was at his weakest, at least physically. Another thing is that even if we are able to resist and the temptation goes away, the demons will be back. After all, Satan left Jesus for a season, not forever. This implies that Satan came back to Jesus, just as he will with us.

When people become depressed, they tend to isolate themselves by withdrawing, not going to church, staying at home, staying in bed, not contacting friends and family, etc. That is just what the demons want us to do. Therefore, it is important for us to fellowship with other Christians, pray, and seek counseling to help remove our emotional garbage so that God's light will shine on us, and we will be in a position to accept and receive His grace and blessings. This will enable us to find our way out. "*Deliver us from evil...*" (Luke 11:2-4). Do not let evil forces isolate you.

Satan cannot tempt what is not in us. That is why it is written, "*Do not let the sun set on your anger nor give place to the Devil,*" (Ephesians 4:26-27). It was Peter's anger, when Jesus told Peter He would die, that gave place to the Devil (Ephesians 4:26-27) and Judas' love of money and spiritual disconnectedness that allowed Satan to enter him (Luke 22:3-6). This is another example of the demonic tactic of *spiritual isolation.* Judas was the only apostle who was not from Galilee. As such, he was considered an outsider by the other eleven. I can imagine that they may not have trusted him, invited him to their functions, or even liked him. Judas also loved money more than the Lord Jesus Christ. This is why he did not like the action of the woman pouring expensive oil on Jesus (Matthew 9:32). He would rather she had sold the oil and given him the money. The fundamental point is that Judas was not in an intimate relationship with the Lord. This is another example of isolation or separation from the Lord.

In addition to handling the apostles' money, Judas was the one sent ahead of Jesus and the apostles to make arrangements for them to sleep and eat as they traveled from town to town. We can imagine that he may not have been present to listen to all of Jesus' teachings. Therefore, Judas was not as physically or spiritually connected to Jesus as the other apostles. All of this was complicated by Judas' love of money. Taken together, we can see that Judas was isolated with circumstances by Satan, who then chose him to arrange the arrest of Jesus for money. *"The Devil had already put into the heart of Judas, the son of Iscariot, the thought of betraying Jesus. As it is written, we cannot serve two masters. We cannot serve God and man/money"* (James 4:4, Matthew 12:30, 6:24, and Luke 11:23).

Demons use this same tactic on Christians today. Like Judas, many of us are in service to Jesus, as are ministers, pastoral counselors, and charity organizations, organizations such as Right to Life, families, and even some churches. These are fine and good works, but when they interfere with worship, or lead to anger, jealousy, misunderstanding, or burnout, they are counter-productive. These activities can become a distraction from worship and, after all, worship is our number one duty. Consider the example of Mary and Martha. When Jesus came to their home, Mary sat with Jesus and the others, listening to and learning from Him, while Martha was in the house preparing the food. Martha came to Jesus and said, *"Tell Mary to help me,"* (Luke 10:40). Jesus responded and said, *"Mary has chosen the more important thing to do,"* (Luke 10:42). It is most important for us to worship and learn. We do not get to heaven by good works, alone. We only get there by worship and accepting Jesus Christ as our Lord and Savior and allowing Him to transform us.

I once had a client who, when discussing his wife, said that she was a very kind and helpful person, often donating her services to other people. But after doing many things for the same person, she would often become bitter. I suggested to him that he tell his wife that she should only give when she was willing to give because when your service becomes a duty, instead of something you want to do of your own free will, it can lead to negative emotions like anger. It is better to do that which will bring you closer to God than man, just as Martha learned (Luke 10:38-42).

## Tactics of a Spiritual Defense

The victory has already been won. When Jesus Christ died on the cross, he won the war for all time. He defeated both death and Satan. But that does not mean that we will not have our own individual battles to fight. That is why it is important that we learn how to rebuke the demons. Look at this example of how Jesus expelled the demons in the case of the madman (Luke 8:26). The apostles came to Jesus and said that they had not been able to expel the demons from this man. When he was tied up, he would always break loose from his bonds, and he would run through the graveyard naked. Jesus told them that some demons have to be expelled through fasting and prayer, as well as by rebuking. This is an important weapon in spiritual warfare, that of rebuking the Devil. Yet not all demons are going to be easily rebuked. They may have a very tight hold on the individual, and in order to get rid of them, as Jesus said, one may need to fast and pray. But Jesus also went on to say that after the demons have been expelled, there will be a void and our house will be swept clean. If we do not fill this void with something that is pure and strong, then the demons will come back even stronger than ever. In fact, according to Matthew 12:43-45, they will return seven times as strong. When this happens, the person will be worse off than he was originally. While in this life, spiritual warfare is never won. It is a continuous battle of trying to stay in the light of God.

Before we continue talking about how we can expel demons, it is good to know who our principal ally is. On our own, we can try to resist the Devil. Certainly the apostles had power to cast out demons. It is through the grace of the Holy Spirit, the Comforter that Jesus sent to the apostles and to us, that we have strength to fight.

So, what is the function of the Holy Spirit? God's guarantee of our salvation through the Holy Spirit can be found in Ephesians 1:14 and 4:30. The Holy Spirit reveals truth (Ephesians 3:5). The Holy Spirit gives us power (Ephesians 3:16). The Holy Spirit gives us a sense of unity (Ephesians 4:3). The Holy Spirit gives us peace (Ephesians 4:3). Our strongest ally, without whom we can do nothing, is the Holy Spirit. Remember that the Holy Spirit is our guarantee of salvation. Without Him, there is no hope of being able to fight off demons. He is God's mark on us. For God has poured out His love into our hearts by means of the Holy Spirit, who is God's gift to us (Romans 5:5).

It has been my experience that the best defense against internal demonic influences is two-fold. First, we should consider psycho-therapy to help identify the source of our emotional battles. Psychotherapy deals with that part of us that is human. Until we get our human nature under control, the Spirit cannot rule. Consider Galatians 5:16:

*What I say is this, let the Spirit direct our lives, and ye will not satisfy the desires of the human nature, for what our human nature wants is opposed to what the Spirit wants, for what the Spirit wants is opposed to what our human nature wants. These two are enemies and this means that you cannot do what you want to do. If the Spirit leads you, then you are not subject to the law. What human nature does is quite plain. It shows itself in immorality, selfish and indecent actions, and the worship of idols and witchcraft. People become enemies, they fight, and they become jealous, angry and ambitious. They separate into parties and groups. They are envious, are drunk, have orgies, and do other things like these. I warn you now as I have before, those who do these things will not possess the Kingdom of God. But the Spirit produces love, joy, peace, patience, kindness, goodness, faithfulness, humility and self-control. And yet there is no law against such things.*

Colossians also speaks about human nature. In Colossians 3:5-9, it says:

*We must put to death then the earthly desires at work in you, such as sexual immorality, indecency, lust, evil passions and greed, for greed is a form of idolatry. Because of such things, God's anger will come upon those who do not obey him. At one time, you, yourselves used to live according to such desires when your life was dominated by them* (meaning evil influences and human nature).

In Ephesians 2:3, we read:

*Actually all of us were like them and lived according to our natural desires doing whatever suited the wishes of our own bodies and minds."* In chapter 4, verse 25, this idea is continued, *"If ye become angry, do not let your anger lead you into sin and do not stay angry all day. Don't give the Devil a chance. The man who used to rob must stop robbing and start working in order to earn an honest living for him and to be able to help the poor. Do not use harmful words, but only helpful words, the kind that build up and provide what is needed so that what you say will be good to those who hear you. And do not make God's Holy Spirit sad, for the Spirit is God's mark of ownership on you, a guarantee that the day will come when God will set you free. Get rid of all bitterness, passion and anger. No more shouting or insults. No more hateful feelings of any sort. Instead be kind and tenderhearted to one another and forgive one another as God has forgiven you through Christ.*

These are some of the things that Christian psychotherapy can help you with in dealing with your human nature and dealing with the things that displease God.

Christian psychotherapy can help expose emotional garbage, give you ways of resolving it, and then go into the next phase of defense against demonic influence, that is, rebuking the Devil. The idea is this: when you are in a fight with somebody else, the first thing you need to do is to get the enemy off yourself — to push the enemy away because you cannot reach for any of your weapons until you get distance between you and the Devil. The best way I know of getting your enemy off is to rebuke the Devil. By rebuking, I am saying something such as this, "Satan and evil spirits, I rebuke you in the name of Jesus Christ, Son of the living God, who was born, died, buried, and rose again the third day." This should give us immediate relief. If you want to get really intense with it, perhaps you could call your demon by its name.

Don't forget, we are talking about spiritual warfare, and in warfare the soldiers have different jobs. Just as with physical warfare, you can have infantrymen, tankers, corpsmen, pilots, sailors, marines, submariners and the like. It takes a lot of beings to fight a war. Many of them have specialized jobs. Think of demons as having specialized jobs, such as demons of hate, demons of despair, demons of anger, demons of helplessness, demons of addiction, demons of lust; the list goes on and on. These demons have colleagues. Just as two or three different aspects of the army may be used to attack a position, such as infantrymen and tank drivers, we can be attacked by two or three different types of demons, such as demons of anger and frustration, or perhaps the demons of anger will team up with the demons of fornication and lust. We may have two or three demons working in concert for our downfall. In this way we can give specialized attention when we rebuke and we can say something like:

"Demons of anger, demons of frustration, demons of lust, demons of helplessness, demons of hopelessness, demons of rape, demons of conceit, I rebuke you in the name of Jesus Christ, Son of the living God, who was born, died, buried, and rose again the third day."

Christian Psychotherapy can help you recognize which demons are working against you. However we rebuke our demons, it will be effective. I have seen it work for people who are angry. I have seen it work for people who are substance abusers. I have seen it work because God is good and God is mighty. After rebuking, then we can pray for protection with something like, "Cover me with the blood of Jesus."

There are behavioral techniques that are related to the concept of filling the void, especially when it comes to the idea of thought insertion. There is the behavioral technique called *self-talk*, the things you say to yourself. When things are going badly, we can unconsciously say negative things to ourselves that facilitate failure. These thought insertions could give the demons a place in your head. It is important to identify those thoughts. Remember that the battle is within our minds. That is the battlefield. After we identify our negative self-talk, it is important to make that self-talk positive. For instance, if you expect to get rejected and say to yourself something like, "Oh, these people will never hire me," chances are you are setting yourself up for a fall and you will cause your own destruction and cause yourself not to be accepted. You have created a self-fulfilling prophecy. It is important to balance this self-talk with something positive like, "I'm sure they will hire me because I have all the qualifications and if they don't hire me, clearly it is their loss," or "If I don't get this job it's because God has something better for me." Another example of negative self-talk might be, "I'm not good enough to go to church. I have nothing to wear. Why bother? I'm late anyway. I can watch it on TV," and things such as that. These are just rudimentary examples of things one should not say.

Another warfare tactic is to protect yourself. You might do this by filling your house with joyful noise like Godly music. Listen to gospel, spiritual, and/or praise music. This will help keep you in an atmosphere of Godliness, to keep yourself surrounded by the joyful music of the Lord. As Paul says in Colossians 3:16:

*Christ's message in all its richness must live in your heart. Teach and instruct one another with all wisdom. Sing songs and hymns, and sacred songs. Sing to God with thanksgiving in your heart. Everything you do or say, then, should be done in the name of the Lord Jesus as you give thanks through Him to God the Father.*

Paul also was singing praises, preaching, and praying when he was imprisoned and was miraculously delivered from the prison (Acts 16:25-28).

In light of the tactic of mind sweep, I would like to share a technique I used successfully. Scripture tells us to *"pray unceasingly"* (Luke 21:36, 18:1, Colossians 4:2, and Ephesians 6:18). There is good reason for this. We are always subject to attack. I have developed the habit of rebuking the Devil, even when I do not feel particularly attacked. For me, this is a way to train my mind to go into rebuking and resisting, as a reflex action when I do not have time to think. When we are under physical attack, we often use reflex actions to protect ourselves. We need to learn to be able to resist and rebuke the Devil as an automatic response.

And lastly, we may also do well to purify our homes, offices, automobiles, or any other structure where we spend extended periods of time. One such method is that of using oil on all windows and doors while rebuking the Devil and asking Jesus for protection. This reminds me of the Passover. In Job 1:10-11, we read that one of the reasons that Satan could not disturb Job was because God blessed all he did and had a hedge of protection around him and his property. We should consider rebuking the demons and asking God to put a hedge around our families and ourselves. Also, Paul says in Ephesians 6:13 that we are to put on the whole armor of God.

## In Conclusion

Much has been discussed in this section on Spiritual Warfare. As I said earlier, we are not human beings with a spiritual side but spiritual beings with a temporary and fragile human side. You must know that whatever you have chosen as your primary identity will direct your path. Understanding your true identity as a spiritual being and child of God will put you on the path to be in concert with God's will. After all, we are commanded to worship God in spirit and truth. You cannot do this if being a human being is your primary identity. Christ left us in the hands and care of the Holy Spirit. We cannot communicate with God unless we acknowledge Him so we can grow in spirit. *"May God the source of hope, fill you with all joy and peace by means of your faith in Him, so that your hope will continue to grow by the power of the Holy Spirit,"* (Romans 15:13). Finally, some detail about spiritual warfare has been discussed.

While many of the trials and tribulations we will experience will have their origins in the spiritual realm, there will also be problems of the physical realm that will be exacerbated by the spiritual. *"And crowds of people came from the towns around Jerusalem, bringing those who were sick or had evil spirits in them; and they were healed"* (Acts 5:16). *"Even handkerchiefs and aprons he [Peter] had used were taken to the sick, and their diseases were driven away, and the evil spirits would go out of them,"* (Acts 19:12). Diseases such as Bipolar Disorder, Schizophrenia, and the like are physical problems that require the professional help of psychologists and psychiatrists. Other problems will be voluntary issues of the flesh. However, some problems are spiritual. You don't have to wonder on which level to fight a problem. Fight them on all levels. All is fair in love and war. We are all at war. For this reason, it is a good idea to be fully dressed and energized to start the day. I suggest you pray first thing in the morning to be spiritually dressed and energized; then do physical exercise to be emotionally and physically energized. Exercise will release endorphins that combat depression. *"Physical exercise has some value, but spiritual exercise is valuable in every way, because it promises life both for the present and for the future"* (1 Timothy 4:8). *"I am the light of the world. Whoever follows me will have the light of life and will never walk in darkness,"* (John 8:12). Stay in the light!

# The Mind

In this part, we will consider what the mind is, where the mind is, and how the mind works. Most importantly we will look at how we can use our minds to bring us to our fullest potential. This chapter consists of three sections:

**Philosophical and Scientific Perspectives.** Here we will look at the mind from scientific and philosophical points of view.

**What Scripture says about the Mind.** In this section, we will examine what Scripture has to say about the mind. My perspective, in this text, is from the Holy Bible. If you are not Christian or do not believe the Bible to be the Word of God, then, for this discussion, at least respect the Bible as a book of wisdom. It is, after all, one of the oldest books in the world.

**Mental Programming.** In this section, I will give you psychological methods designed to train the mind to enhance and enrich your life. This motivational section is not dependent on Christian belief.

## Philosophical and Scientific Perspectives

For ages, scientists have wondered about the mind. No one knows for sure where intelligence, decision making, perception, awareness, and sense of self reside. Where is the mind located? How does it work? Does it result from the electro-chemical processes of the brain, or is this something ethereal that might be closer to the spiritual concept of the soul?

Thinkers have pondered the question of the mind ever since time began. Plato believed the mind to be located in the head. For him, the sphere was the highest geometrical form, so the mind must be located in the head, which is somewhat spherical in shape. Aristotle felt the mind was located in the heart. He reasoned the warmth of blood is our life force, so the mind must be there also. By the Middle Ages, conventional wisdom agreed that the mind was located in the brain. This belief persists even to this day. In the 17th century, a French philosopher, Rene Descartes, said, "While the mind may live in the brain, it is a non-material thing, entirely separate from the physical tissues found inside the head." Descartes also coined the phrase, "I think, therefore I am." One way of understanding this statement is that "consciousness is the only evidence we exist" (Time, 7/17/95 "In Search of the Mind").

Powerful modem technology, such as magnetic resonance imaging tomography (MRI) and positron-emission tomography (PET), has allowed scientists to trace the process of sight from the retina, which is part of the eye, to deep inside the brain; and watch a thought such as fear burst from the section of the brain called the amygdala, and the resultant finding of neurons as a long buried memory is resurrected. This technology is helping us close the gap between the thinking of ancient Greek philosophers and modern day scientists. That is, we now know that the mind is not a physical thing that we can touch, see, or smell. Also, the mind and brain are not usually separate from each other.

Scientists conclude that processes of the mind, such as consciousness, are much more complicated than previously imagined. They agree that Descartes was right when he said the mind is not a physical thing, and while it resides in the brain, it has no particular location; however, Descartes was wrong about the mind and brain being wholly independent of each other. Input from the senses, body chemicals, memory, and language are all facilitated by the mind /brain interaction.

In September 1999, I saw a documentary on TV about a middle-aged, conservative parent, and former dancer who received the nation's first heart and lung transplants. Her donor was a 21-year-old male who had died in a motorcycle accident. Subsequent to her surgery, she began to notice profound changes in some of her behaviors. She suddenly had cravings for beer and chicken nuggets. This was something she had never experienced before. Additionally, her handwriting changed from a right slant to a left slant. The woman located and spoke to the parents of her donor and discovered that beer and chicken nuggets had been favorites of their son and that he had written with a backward slant. Doctors explained this phenomenon by saying each cell of our body has memory capabilities. Perhaps the mind is all over the body and only headquartered in the brain.

Even with a wide variety of theories and hypotheses, scientists still cannot determine where or what the mind is or is not. It may be that scientists will never know for sure and may have to admit that the mind, which has no physical existence, may just be God's breath of life or the soul.

## What Scripture says about the Mind

The mind is that mental capacity that allows us to think. In the previous section, Spiritual Warfare, I discussed my hypothesis that not all thoughts that come into your head are necessarily yours. At this point, however, we will deal with thoughts that are yours and originate with self.

To get a glimpse of how important the mind is, let's see what God has to say about it. We are commanded to love God with all our hearts and all our minds (Matthew 22:37). Scripture also tells us the benefits of a good mind. Paul describes three ideal states of mind in Philippians.

**The single-mind:** one purpose of fighting together for the faith and gospel (Philippians 1: 27).

**The spiritual-mind:** we should share love, not be selfish and be humble (Philippians 2:2 & 3).

**The secure-mind:** a secure mind receives the peace of God (Philippians 4:7).

The profound relationship between the mind and the will of God, which is mediated by the spirit, is also found in scripture: *"Be ye transformed by the renewing of your mind, that ye may prove what is good, and acceptable, and the perfect will of God"* (Romans 12:1-2). Listen to what God says about those who do not have a good mind. *"Go and say to these people: you will listen and listen, but not understand; you will look and look, but not see, because your minds are dull, and you have stopped up your ears and closed your eyes. Otherwise, your eyes would see, your ears would hear, your minds would understand, and you would turn to me, says God, and I will heal you"* (Acts 28:26-27). I might add that this passage is so important it is repeated at least four times (Matthew 13:14-15, John 12:40, Acts 28:26-27, and Isaiah 6:9-10).

It is, of course, good to do things with the mind. However, there are times when the mind is not employed in our actions. Such times would be when we act on impulse or reflex. These situations can occur when we are angry, fearful, or even in lust and not in love.  Lust is a physical instinctive reaction while love should be the result of the heart acting in concert with the mind. This is discussed in more detail in the next section, Relationships.  We get a glimpse of how the mind works from Scripture if we consider the parable of the Sower (Matthew 13:1-18).  In it, Jesus describes how seeds fall on different parts of the field such as along the path, on rocky ground, among thorn bushes, and in good soil. For me, the field is the mind. It is, therefore, up to us to sow and/or accept good seeds in our minds. Our mind, like the field, will grow whatever is planted. Plant seed in good soil. We can plant good seed and God will plant seeds/thoughts in our minds (Romans 2:2, Matthew 16:23).

Thought, a major function of the mind, can be in the form of words, concepts, or pictures. We will refer to the latter as visions. Scripture teaches us that a people without vision are lost (Proverbs 29:18). What is vision? For our purposes, vision is a hope for a thing unseen, a picture of expectations for a future event such as a vision of being with Christ when we die, prosperity, etc. The fulfillment of visions requires faith in God and ourselves.

## Science versus Scripture

Thus far, we have looked at the mind from both scientific and scriptural points of view. As sophisticated as our modern technology is, we cannot locate the mind. As wise as the Greek and French philosophers were, they were really only speculating. We know a lot about the brain, but the brain is not synonymous with the mind. It is brain chemistry that controls emotions and directs behavior. While we can trace the biological activity of thoughts in the brain, there is no evidence that conclusively says thoughts originate in the brain.

Scripture suggests the mind is the most crucial part in understanding; apparently, it is not just the brain. If your mind is sharp, you will comprehend and understand God's will for your life and the world around you. Also, anything planted in the brain will grow if planted in the good soil of the mind. For me, good soil of the mind is a mind directed by the Holy Spirit. This is like the difference between wisdom and knowledge. Wisdom is from God. Knowledge is from man. A case in point was in a TV documentary about Albert Einstein. He said his discoveries in the science of physics were his attempt to read the mind of God and that is where he received his inspiration.

It would be ridiculous to think that God would create us without a mind. We are created in His image. Angels, who have limited knowledge, probably have a mind. Because the brain is a material thing, I doubt angels have a brain. My point is that while there is an intimate connection between the mind and the brain, the mind is God's gift to us that makes us in His image. The mind is not a by-product of brain functioning. I suspect the mind is the soul or at least an integral part of it. The mind does not need the brain to exist. I believe the mind exists after death. Because I believe in an eternal soul, I feel the mind and soul are one and the same.

## Mental Programming

Long before I considered a career in psychology, I was using methods described in a branch of psychology referred to as Cognitive Behavioral Therapy. As I further investigated this style, I found that many great athletes and corporate executives have also used variations of this type of psychology to motivate and energize themselves and their employees because it is efficient and effective. This is not mind over matter but a method of mental programming that maximizes human and spiritual potential.

The first time I unwittingly used Cognitive Behavioral Therapy was when I wanted to buy a new car. In 1980 I wanted a Pontiac Firebird Trans Am. At that time, the Firebird Trans Am had a big eagle painted on the hood. I went to the car dealer, but he would not approve my credit. It never occurred to me that I would not get the needed financing to purchase this car, so I saw the dealer's refusal to advance me credit as a minor setback. I thanked him and asked for some color brochures of the car. I went home and cut out pictures of the car, put them on walls all over the house, and focused on them. I imagined this car parked in front of my house, picked a color, imagined myself driving it, and all my friends admiring it. Two weeks later, I went to another dealer and was successful in buying the car.

The next time I used this method was to get my doctorate degree. Before I tell you about this, I need to give you some background about my academic situation. When I was in kindergarten, the teacher told my mother I was retarded. They wanted to make me repeat the grade, but my mother told them to promote me. During the first or second grade, my mother was told if I got past the eighth grade, it would be a minor miracle. It wasn't that I was failing, but I just barely got by with C's. There are many reasons why a teacher would say this. It could have been racism; I may have had Attention Deficit Hyperactivity Disorder (ADHD), poor academic motivation, or simply been too immature (my parents started me in kindergarten at the age of 3).

It was shortly after this that my mother enrolled my brother, sister, and me in a parochial school. Grade school was uneventful, and I was an average student. However, I had more problems in high school. I was 12 years old in the 9th grade and the only Black male in the class. Although I was never an honor roll student, I did OK. At the age of 16, in my senior year of high school, my homeroom teacher told me, "Any college that accepts you is hard-up." Needless to say, I was crushed. I passed all of my classes. However, in Math, I delighted in correcting the teacher, to her embarrassment. The same year, my father told me I was too stupid to finish high school and that I should drop out and get a job. When I was an adult, I confronted my father and asked him why he had said this. He told me he hoped this would motivate me to do better. I told him it didn't work. At any rate, no one but my mother was taking any bets on me. Most mothers are good for unconditional positive regard. My mom's love, faith, and vision for my success is the foundation of my life achievements. However, my self-image was damaged.

After 10 years of being out of high school, which included four years in the Air Force, I was working as a self-employed plumber. My girlfriend, Karen, thought I was intelligent and encouraged me to attend college. However, I decided to take a refresher course first. The Black Muslim community in Boston offered a free pre-college course. During that course, my math teacher told me how brilliant I was. My entire high-school math curriculum, including algebra, geometry, trigonometry, and calculus, came flooding into my mind and brain.

When I finished this course, the Muslim preparatory school helped me secure an affirmative action scholarship to the Massachusetts College of Pharmacy. I wasn't particularly interested in becoming a pharmacist, but this was the only school they could get me into, so I took the opportunity. On the entrance exam my reading score was at the level of a college freshman. It was then that it occurred to me that I was not dumb.

During my freshman year at the Massachusetts College of Pharmacy, four other affirmative action students and I walked into the Mathematics class. The teacher said the class would not be able to move as quickly as before because of us. Halfway through the semester, the teacher made another announcement. He said he had to stop giving extra credit questions on his tests because they were not fair to me. My average was 115 and the highest grade he could give me was A. My grade was better than that. At the College of Pharmacy, I was also the class president. The scholarship ran out after two years. I was now sure I didn't want to be a pharmacist, but the Sociology classes I took there interested me. I decided to pursue my interest in mental health at a local community college. I transferred to Roxbury Community College, which was my first experience with an all Black school. I blossomed. Here, I earned a 4.0 average and graduated first of 500 students. From here, I enrolled in the University of Massachusetts, where I concentrated in psychology. During my time there I made the Dean's list even though I took a double load of subjects and ran a plumbing business that employed four people. This was also about the time I met my wife, Maxine.

I graduated from the University of Massachusetts in 1977, applied to graduate school, and matriculated at the Massachusetts School of Professional Psychology. Again I was the only Black. When I first started graduate school, I did an internship at a state mental health hospital. While there, another intern asked to give me an IQ test as practice for him. I consented. I scored in the Bright-Normal range of intellectual functioning. During the time of my studies there, I took a Psychophysiology course. Even though the school operated on a pass/fail system, my professor insisted on giving me an A. My self-confidence was building. I imagined myself as a doctor. I do not say this to brag but to point out how sometimes when others, who are important to you, try to pull you down by planting bad seed in the garden of your mind, you can overcome it by planting your own positive seeds in conjunction with anything anyone has ever said that was positive. I do not know why the professor insisted on giving me an A, but this and my IQ score served as positive seeds to combat the negative seeds others had planted. Prior to this, it was my mother and me against my father, grade school teachers, and that one high school teacher.

In graduate school, I was once again the only Black. The school was 90% Jewish. I mention this because this was my first experience of feeling colorless. I was like family. The love I experienced there helped me as much as the education. However the main reason I mention it is because you may find that to get to where you want to be, you must traverse uncharted waters alone, that is, without familiar surroundings or people. Of course, familiar surroundings can be comfortable, but they can act as either help or a hindrance. They can help because they can make you feel comfortable and supported; however, they can also make you lazy or complacent. Unfamiliar surroundings can be uncomfortable, but the anxiety created can stimulate growth and development.

In both instances, buying my first new car and earning my doctorate degree, I used a technique called *visualization*. This is one of the many techniques used in Cognitive Behavior Therapy. As mentioned earlier, envisioning and planting ideas is a function of the mind facilitated by the brain.

With hindsight and the knowledge gained as a psychologist, an analysis of the crucial elements of my accomplishments proved to me that the result of visualization is fulfillment. Visualizations were used to program my mind for success. After all, Christ said, *"If you have the faith of a mustard seed and say mountain move, it will move,"* if it is God's will (Matthew 17:20).

The particular seeds I have been describing involve self-esteem. All of the negative things people had said to me, as a child, tended to make me feel bad about myself. For this reason, I would like to share 7 steps to improve your self-esteem. These are useful when used in conjunction with Matthew 17:20. Walter Anderson, a teacher of self-confidence, delineated "The Seven Pillars of Confidence." They are paraphrased as follows: (Lauren Picker, Self Magazine, 1996).

1.  **Accept Responsibility for Your Own Happiness and Sadness.** We are not only the products of genetics and environment, but more importantly, we are products of the choices we make in life. When I was a child, my father asked how an object got broken. I said, "It broke." He said, "It can't do anything." I told him, "I broke it." By questioning me, he forced me to take responsibility for my actions and the consequences. This means that if you are poor, in a bad marriage, or in any way dissatisfied with your life, it is the result of choices you have made. When you accept responsibility for your life, then, and only then, can you change it. *"When I was a child, I thought as a child"* (1 Corinthians 13:1). If I received a poor grade on my report card, I would say the teacher gave me a C. By doing this, I was putting my destiny in the hands

of others instead of accepting the responsibility for my future and destiny.

2. **Make Anxiety Your Ally.** Anxiety is the human response to anticipated danger. However, it is also an energizer. Psychological studies have shown that moderate levels of anxiety heighten cognitive ability, but when anxiety becomes overwhelming, it can impede thought. In this situation, you can pray and/or take 10 deep breaths. Inhale through your nose while pushing your stomach out and exhale through your mouth. Then charge forward.

3. **Compete to Improve Yourself.** To get better at anything, you must compete with those who are better than you. We learn from those who know more than we do. For example, to make yourself better, you have to play with those who are better.

4. **Recognize Mistakes as Opportunities.** Anderson suggests using his R.I.P. acronym. **R** - *responsibility.* Take responsibility for your mistakes. Don't ignore them; learn from them. **I** - *insight.* Study the mistake so you can gain knowledge from the experience. **P** - *perspective.* Although mistakes can be humiliating and hurtful, try not to take it too personally. We all make mistakes.

Success is always the result of failed attempts. Edison failed in over 1000 attempts before he invented the light bulb. Walt Disney went bankrupt 7 times before he was successful. When I was 17, my father took me to the airport to catch a plane to Texas where I did my Air Force basic training. On the way, he gave me my first piece of positive advice, telling me something I did not fully understand until I was in my late 20's. He said, "Son, if what you are doing does not work, do something else. It is better to make a new mistake than to keep making the same old mistakes over and over again. Only a fool keeps making the same mistake. Son, go out there and find yourself a new mistake." The part I did not get right away was if all of your mistakes are new, then you have learned from it. That is, try to profit from your mistakes and experiences.

5.  **Be Brave.** In a book by Eleanor Roosevelt, <u>You Learn By Living</u>, she states, "You gain courage and strength by every experience in which you really stop to look fear in the face. Then you can say to yourself, I lived through this horror. I can take the next thing that comes along. You must do the thing you cannot do." Real confidence is born of experience, and getting that experience often means forging ahead even if you are afraid. Courage is the ability to act in spite of fear. Anything worth having is not only difficult but can also cause you to be afraid. If your objective is worth it, you are supposed to be a little or a lot nervous.

So what if you're afraid? Anderson suggests that you adapt an idea from the Delancy Street Foundation, a highly successful rehabilitation program in San Francisco for criminal offenders. Their fundamental principle is "Act as If". Former drug abusers, prostitutes, and convicts are told to act as if they care about other people even if they do not. Eventually, they actually begin to develop empathy. So, act as if you're brave, and before long you will not just be acting, you will feel courageous. "Act as If" forces you to focus on solutions. Right thinking is followed by right actions. *From out of the abundance of the heart, the mouth speaks.*

When you say, "How do I act as if I'm brave?" "How do I act as if I am confident?", you force yourself to focus on solutions. Asking these questions will provide the answers. You will never get answers if you do not ask questions. If you ask the wrong questions, you will receive the wrong answers. Ask the right questions and you are likely to get the right answers/solutions. This technique incorporates two Behavioral Therapy techniques. One is that you put the behavior before the feelings. Unlike Psychodynamic Theory, which is based on the idea that if you change feelings, behavior will follow, Behavioral Theory postulates that if you change the behavior, feelings will follow. While one technique is not necessarily better than the other, it has been my professional experience that behavioral techniques are generally faster than dynamic techniques. The other behavioral technique incorporated in the above-mentioned issue is that of *self-talk*. It is theorized that we often set ourselves up by what we say to ourselves. This is similar to a self-fulfilling prophecy. If you say self-defeating things to yourself, you are more likely to fail. If you say encouraging things to yourself, you are more likely to succeed. As Paul says, we should think on things that are of good report (Philippians 4:8).

6. **Be Ambitious.** In order to be ambitious, you have to have specific goals. Do not let barriers or setbacks limit what you can become. Also remember, who you are is different from what you are or what you have. Patterning your life after others can be unfulfilling. If you allow others to define who you are, you will always be dependent on others for your identity. Your identity is who you are. Whoever defines your identity controls your destiny. Pursue your own dreams. Even better would be to pursue God's plan for your life. He has a plan for all of us.

7. **Take Risks.** One type of risk is positive loss, the loss of innocence or ignorance. This becomes apparent when you realize you are not satisfied with your present circumstance, be it a job, relationship, etc. Another type of risk is practical loss; this is what you sacrifice to get ahead. To go to college, you might have to give up socializing with friends. When

considering any risk, define a clear goal. Review the positive and practical losses. When you focus on risks with a larger purpose or goal, you are on the right track. Act. Take a risk.

**Be confident.** To get to where you want to be, you must accept responsibility, believe in something big, practice tolerance, be brave, be ambitious, and smile. No one else can do it for you.

## Motivation

Thoughts are representative of who we are, and they emanate from the mind not the brain. Thoughts activate the brain to control our feelings. Negative thoughts have been linked to all kinds of illnesses. Positive thoughts have been associated with better health, habits, and accomplishments. For instance, let's look at depression. Depression can be reduced to two types, indogenous and exogenous.

Indogenous depression emanates from inside the brain. It can be the result of an inherited predisposition and/or brain chemistry. These types include Bipolar Disorder or Manic Depression, Cyclothymia (change of season), and Hypomania (thyroid condition), to name a few.

Exogenous depressions are largely situational. That is, they are not initiated by brain chemistry, as is the former group, but are facilitated by environmental situations such as grief over the loss of a loved one, losing a job, etc. This second type of depression has been shown to be largely due to, or a by-product of, maladaptive thinking and can be successfully treated with mental training. Paul speaks on this topic using what I feel is a form of mental training and imagery. "*In conclusion, my brothers, fill your minds with those things that are good and deserve praise, things that are true, noble, right, pure, lovely, and honorable,*" (Philippians 4:8). This is an example of Bible psychology which psychologists call cognitive restructuring.

Our thoughts and mental images can determine our feelings and behavior. This is an integral part of the gift of free will that God the Father has given us. It would not make sense for God to give us free will and leave our destiny in the hands of fate or luck. Christ died that we might have abundant life both now and for eternity. We will discuss just how we can train our minds to overcome depression and other problems when I address programming your mind. For now, we will continue in our discussion of the importance of vision and other expectations for the future.

Our vision for the future can come from the past or present. Family members such as a spouse, parents, teachers, priests, ministers or any other important persons in our lives help shape it. Mental input that we accept can be like the seed mentioned earlier or like a tape that plays over and over again convincing us of its validity. If a teacher or parent called you stupid, you may still believe it. To actualize our brainwashing, we act in accordance with our beliefs, resulting in a self-fulfilling prophecy.

There was a famous psychological experiment where teachers were told that randomly selected children were exceptionally bright. They were, in fact, of just average ability. The teachers believed the psychologists and, in their expectation of high intelligence of the children, treated them differently. These children thrived and got very good grades, upholding the idea that we get what we expect. (Pygmalion in the Classroom: Teacher Expectation and Pupils' Intellectual Development, Rosenthal and Jacobson). People will often raise or lower themselves to the level of what their significant others expect. Faith and visualization allow us to rise to the level of our own and/or others' expectations.

When my daughter was in high school, I taught her a variation of this mindset. I told her if she studied hard, right from the beginning of the school year, and earned an A, her teachers would see her as an A student. If she later wrote a B paper, teachers would still be likely to give her an A and relegate her B paper as the result of having a bad day or some such thing. It worked then and it continues to work now. In her senior year of college, she had a 4.0 average. The best aspect about this way of thinking is that it has increased my daughter's self-confidence and grade point average, making this a win/win situation.

The importance of the mind in determining success or failure is further illustrated in the April 24, 1996, issue of the *New Journal & Guide*, in which an article by James E. Alsbrook illustrates the importance of mindset. His article is entitled "Black Students Bloom Equally When Free." Professor Steele, a black professor at the University of Michigan, ran a race-based experiment. He found that when white students were told that Asian students were better in mathematics, the white students' scores dropped and the Asian students' scores increased. He went on to point out that when Black freshmen's SAT scores were compared to whites, the Blacks scored 100 points lower; however, after one year in a special program, the Black participants caught up.

The problem that afflicted whites in their math test scores with Asians and afflicted Blacks in their SAT scores as compared to whites is a psychological reaction now called stereotype threat. It is proof that we perform according to our mindsets.

"The mind's double-edge power is at work in all of us, either hindering and making us miserable or facilitating our efforts and making us feel good. Your mind keeps you from doing things it does not believe are possible, but once it accepts that you can do it, (provided of course, that you are prepared in other ways), the mind will provide a way. Motivation, competitiveness, confidence, will, perseverance, and belief in self are all qualities of the mind" (Mind Power by Zilbergeld & Lazarus).

## Programming the Mind

The natural inclination of the mind is to satisfy the desires of the flesh to receive immediate gratification. However, if we are to follow the will of God, set goals, and strive for success, we need to learn how to train the mind. The process of mental training does this. Mental training is simply a way of re-programming the mind to achieve more positive behaviors, feelings, and results. How the mind perceives and interprets information determines what you think, how you feel, and what you do.

There are three basic components of mental training: 1) setting goals, 2) creating a relaxed and receptive state of mind, and 3) instituting positive suggestion.

### Goal Setting

It is impossible to get where you're going or accomplish great things if you don't know where you are going or what you want out of life. Without a goal, you are subject to the winds of fate or someone else's dreams, for example, that of your employer. Your employer has his own dream and specific goals. This person is focused and you are helping make his dreams come true. As long as you are making his dreams come true, you might as well have dreams of your own. After all, the two are not mutually exclusive.

First, you must have an ultimate or long-range goal that is a major accomplishment you feel would make you happy, satisfied, or worthwhile. Although it can be a process such as being a better parent or being happier, it is easier to measure progress if your goal is concrete. Your goal can be something measurable such as achieving wealth, owning your own company, improving your physical health, losing weight, owning a house, getting a college degree, being comfortable around your boss, etc. Spend some time thinking/brainstorming if you don't have a goal. When you are able to focus on a single, measurable long-range goal, write it down.

After you have determined your goal, the next step is to draft a mission statement. To reach your goal, you will need to be on a mission, which is the reason you want to reach your goal. This is very important to do because it will serve as motivation to keep you going when the going gets tough. A mission to be wealthier can be to leave your family an inheritance, to buy a house for your parents, to finance your children's education, etc. The mission to have eternal life is often what motivates people to believe in God. The importance of the mission statement toward achieving goals cannot be understated.

After you have specified in your mission statement why you want to reach your goal, you should define short-range goals. These are the stepping-stones or means by which you intend to reach your ultimate goal. They are also a mechanism by which we can measure our progress toward our long-range goal, something like keeping score. For instance, if you wanted to start your own business, short-range goals could include taking a business course at a local college, having a financial consultation, renting an office, and securing a loan. If getting better grades in school is your ultimate goal, then working with a tutor, setting specific study times, and prioritizing activities may be short-term goals. Giving yourself rewards along the way can be useful in helping you look forward to completing each step.

### Creating a Relaxed and Receptive State of Mind

The second component of mental training is relaxation. Relaxation is a type of trance where one is susceptible to suggestion. It is not necessarily hypnosis. We can be in a light trance when we are unaware of external reality. The right side of the brain facilitates this state of mind. Whereas the left-brain is more concerned with external reality, analysis, and logic, the right brain deals more with symbolic thought and the subconscious. This side of the brain is more susceptible to suggestion. To achieve this state, some people engage in various relaxation techniques such as deep breathing, imagery, or deep muscle relaxation.

Relaxation is one method of receptivity. Another is a heightened state of awareness. This can be accomplished when a therapist suggests that an individual be more aware of his or her energy by meditation, with focus on a mantra or spontaneous experiences, such as when one is totally focused on a task like reading. At times such as these, one is startled when interrupted because his total attention is focused. Perhaps the most natural state of focused attention is experienced during sexual intercourse, when having an orgasm.

In terms of mental training, what we will do here is use relaxation with imagery as a method of receptivity to achieve an altered state of consciousness. Psychologically, an altered state of consciousness refers to not being aware or concerned with external reality, that is, to minimize left-brain functioning.

The mind is never still. It is easy to verify this by simply trying to clear your mind of all thought. It is virtually impossible. Even when we sleep, the mind is at work. This work is in the form of dreams. Sleep has various phases. The phase of sleep where there is much mental activity is referred to as REM sleep. REM stands for rapid eye movement. This is when we dream. Whether we remember our dreams or not, all of us dream. This is evidence that the mind is always working.

When we are awake, the mind is constantly telling us things that have been programmed into us. Many of us spend much of our time telling ourselves negative things that make us feel bad, inadequate, or unworthy. "The effectiveness of negative suggestion in bringing about negative results is powerful testimony to the strength of mental training. Imagine negative outcomes often enough and negative outcomes are what you'll get. The good news is that positive suggestion also works. Imagine positive outcomes often enough, in a receptive state, and what you imagine will tend to be what you will get. The therapeutic use of mental training lies precisely in using positive suggestion to the best effect" (Mind Power by Zilbergeld & Lazarus). If you imagine yourself as a winner often enough, you will start to act like one, be treated like one, and become one.

## Mental Training

We will now put all of the aforementioned concepts together to set your goals. First you need to get relaxed. You will do this with a simple relaxation method. Remember the reason for this is so you can activate the right brain, where creativity is resident. The method you will use is called deep breathing relaxation. Inhale through your nose while expanding your diaphragm. That is, push out your stomach while inhaling through your nose. When you do this, hold your breath for 5 seconds, exhale through your mouth, and then give a little push to exhale everything. You will do this 10 times.

Have another person read the following script until you memorize it. Here we go! Place your hand on your stomach:

> Inhale through your nose, hold it, and exhale, and push a little more air out. Very good, now again.
>
> Inhale. Hold it. Exhale. Push a little more air out. You're doing great!
>
> Inhale. Hold it. Exhale all tension. Push a little more out. Great!
>
> Inhale. Hold it. Exhale all anxiety. It is all right to close your eyes if you like.
>
> Inhale. Hold it. Exhale all doubt. You should now begin to feel more relaxed.
>
> Inhale. Hold it. Exhale. Push a little more out.
>
> Inhale. Hold it. Exhale all frustration. Push a little more out.

*Inhale. Hold it. Exhale all anger. Push a little more.*

*Inhale. Hold it. Exhale.*

*Inhale. Think about what you would like to do with your life even if you will not be paid to do it. Hold it. Exhale.*

*Inhale. Remember your dreams of what you love to do. Hold it. Exhale.*

*Inhale. Smile. Hold it. Exhale. Push a little more.*

OK, you should now feel relaxed. Take a piece of paper and write down a major goal. Good! Now write down why you want to reach this goal. This will become your mission statement. In order for us to have a way to measure progress toward this goal, write down three to five things it would take, in ascending order, to reach this goal. If you are not able to do this right now, do the deep breathing exercise again and try to get your goals on paper. Display this paper in a prominent place, look at it every day, and start by doing the easiest step first and progress upward toward the most difficult. It may be helpful to share your goal with a friend who can help motivate you. You may also want to impose a time limit to accomplish each step.

## Instituting Positive Suggestion
The next tactic I want to share with you is that of programming your mind for success. These techniques are called changing perspective and structure of your imagery, recalling past successes, imagining the results, imagining the process, positive talk, and posthypnotic suggestion.

Let me remind you why we are doing this. It is my belief that our spirit or soul programs the mind and visa versa because the mind and spirit are either one and the same or intrinsically interconnected. This being so, the mind will grow anything that is planted. If we plant bad seed, we get weeds. If we plant good seeds, we get flowers. You not only get what you plant, you reap what you sow (Galatians 6:7&8). If negative thoughts are planted, demons guide us to disaster. If we plant positive and Godly thoughts, the Holy Spirit guides us to prosperity. Therefore, mental programming is the planting of seeds.

First, you need to practice relaxation every day. This should take about 15 minutes. Think about it. If anger, anxiety, frustration, and other states of tension attract demons to us, then it makes sense that a state of calm and relaxation can facilitate positive and Godly thoughts. Scripture admonishes, "*Do not let the sun set on your anger nor give place to the Devil,*" (Ephesians 4:26-27). Relaxation cannot be forced but must be allowed to happen. Relaxation is the art of doing nothing and allowing something to happen. Relaxation puts you in the state of mind that makes you receptive to suggestion by activating right-brain functioning. Besides that, it makes you feel good.

Here are four scripts from The Mind Power, p. 101. They are designed to help you quickly achieve a relaxed state of mind. Try all of them and choose the one that works best for you. Make a tape recording of your script and practice it daily for about a week. You should then choose a cue word that will allow you to go into a relaxed state without going through the whole relaxation technique. Your cue word can be anything you want such as Jesus, relax, calm, beach, or mountains.

Before you begin, take as much time as you need to get really settled and comfortable. Find the best position for your body as you begin to let go of tension and enter ever-deeper levels of comfort and relaxation. (Most people find that they relax more deeply with their eyes closed.) Remember, this is a time for your pleasure, for your comfort, for yourself.

## Script 1
## Relaxation via Deep Breathing and Relaxing Imagery
### *Time required: 7 to 10 minutes*

When you feel settled and comfortable, take several deep, satisfying breaths. For the breaths to be as relaxing as possible, it's important that they be deep and satisfying, but without any kind of effort or hassle. Filling your lungs will cause your stomach to protrude a bit. When your lungs are full, hold your breath a moment or two, but not to the point of discomfort. When you feel like it, and only when you feel like it, exhale slowly and comfortably, allowing the air to carry away any tensions you have with it, disappearing into the air — a deep, satisfying exhalation. Then when you are ready, take another deep, satisfying breath, bringing in fresh, life giving air, breathing out stale, tense air, carrying your tensions with it, leaving you feeling lighter, calmer, more relaxed.

When you are ready, take the first of nine or ten really satisfying breaths. You need to leave enough time to take these breaths, but silence is neither necessary nor advisable. As you take the breaths, listen to the following words, or variations on them, leave pauses between them, to encourage your deepening relaxation.

**Note:** I recommend that you read the entire script through at least once before beginning to familiarize yourself with the technique. If you choose to make a tape, record only the italicized portions of the script.

*With each exhalation, imagine tension leaving your body, going out with the air, leaving you feeling more comfortable, more serene, really nice. That's right, more and more relaxed. Tension going out, relaxation coming in. And when you're done with nine or ten deep, satisfying breaths, you can either breathe normally or, take a few more deep, satisfying, and relaxing breaths.*

*To help you relax even further, just let yourself use your mind, that powerful tool that is so helpful in relaxing and making changes that you desire. As you sit there comfortably relaxed, imagine a relaxing scene.*

Here you should use a scene that is relaxing to you. We use the example of lying on a beach. If this works for you, use it; otherwise, use your own scene and give suggestions, as we do, to encourage imagining it as clearly as possible. If you choose a beach scene, use the name of the beach.

*Imagine lying on your blanket on a beautiful beach and as you do, allow yourself to relax even further. Feel the warming rays of the sun on your head, your back, your legs. Feel the blanket under you, warm and comforting. Can you hear the waves breaking, one after the other? Smell the hot dogs cooking and the salty smell of the sea in the air. How comforting and pleasant it is to be on the beach, with nothing to do, nowhere to go, just relaxing, just being. And as you imagine being on the beach, just being and relaxing, allow yourself as much comfort and as much pleasure as you can, letting go, just lying there. There's nothing to do and nowhere to go, so you might as well enjoy and relax — that's very nice.*

Allow yourself to enjoy the pleasant moment as long as you want. Maybe you're realizing that it's not so bad to be fully relaxed and comfortable. Now, let your mind come up with a word or phrase that represents this nice, safe, pleasant feeling. You can pick out your cue word or phrase ahead of time or when listening to the tape. It might be "relaxed." "calm," "serene," "safe," or some combination of these words. It doesn't make any difference as long as the word(s) are associated with the wonderful feeling of relaxation.

*Good. Now, repeat your cue word or phrase every time you exhale. Repeat it several times to yourself. With some practice, when you say your cue word, it will bring back the warm, relaxed, safe feelings you're now experiencing. Do it one more time. Repeat your cue word several times, each time feeling the wonderful relaxing feelings that go with it. Very good.*

When you feel you're finished with the experience and want to come back to your everyday consciousness, just count backwards to yourself from five to one, feeling more alert, more awake with each number.

*Five . . . Four, more alert . . . Three . . . halfway there . . . Two, eyes starting to open . . . One . . . your eyes will be open, you'll be refreshed, awake, fully alert, and still relaxed. You may want to wiggle around a bit to reorient yourself.*

**Script 2:**
**Relaxation by Sensory Awareness**
*Time required: 5 minutes*
Once you are comfortable, listen very closely to the questions you will be asked. Each question can be answered with yes or no. It is not necessary for you to answer aloud. There is no right or wrong answer. What is important is your reaction to the question. Do not bother about the unusual nature of some of the questions. Let yourself react to each question. However you react is fine. Remember, allow your own reaction to be your guide.

- Is it possible for you to allow your eyes to close?

- If your eyes are closed, is it possible for you to keep them closed throughout the remainder of these questions?

- Is it possible for you to imagine the space between your eyes?

- Is it possible for you to imagine the distance between your ears?

- Is it possible for you to become aware of your breathing?

- Is it possible for you to imagine that you are looking at something that is far away in the distance?

- Is it possible for you to notice a warm feeling somewhere in your body?

- Is it possible for you to be aware of where your arms are in contact with the chair?

- If your feet are resting on the floor, can you feel the floor beneath them?

- Is it possible for you to imagine the space within your mouth?

- Is it possible for you to be aware of one of your arms being more relaxed than the other?

- Is it possible for you to be aware of one of your legs being more relaxed than the other?

- Is it possible for you to notice a relaxed feeling some-where inside your body?

- Is it possible for you to feel even the slightest breeze against your cheek?

- Is it possible for you to be aware of the position of your tongue within your mouth?

- Is it possible for your entire body to feel pleasantly heavy and calm?

- Is it possible for you to imagine a beautiful flower sus-pended a few feet in front of you?

Now just allow yourself to be as relaxed and peaceful as you like. Enjoy this feeling for as long as you desire . . . And if they're not yet open, you may open your eyes now and feel wide-awake and yet relaxed and comfortable.

**Script 3:**
**Relaxation by Letting Go**
*Time required: 10 to 12 minutes*
For this exercise, you need to lie or sit so that all parts of your body are supported. You should not have to tense any muscles for any reason. Once you are comfortable, take in a very deep breath. Fill your lungs and hold your breath for a few moments. Exhale and continue breathing normally — in and out. Try to sense a definite calming sensation beginning to develop.

Focus on the feelings in your forehead and scalp. Feel your forehead smoothing out as a wave of relaxation spreads throughout your head, face, neck, and throat. Let your lips part slightly as your jaw relaxes. Allow your tongue to rest comfortably in your mouth as you observe the pleasant feelings of relaxation in your throat and neck area.

As you continue letting go, feel the relaxation spreading down your right arm so that your arm feels pleasantly heavy. Now focus on your right hand and let go of whatever tensions might be there. Feel your right arm relaxing, becoming pleasantly heavy, from your shoulders all the way down to your fingertips. You may feel a tingling sensation. You may experience a feeling of floating. These are signs that tight muscles are loosening. While you continue letting go of the tension in your right arm and hand, turn your attention to your left arm, and allow the relaxation to spread down your left arm and into your left hand. Just let it go further and further. Now your head, jaw, and face are relaxed, your neck and throat are relaxed, your shoulders and arms are relaxed, all the way down to the tips of your fingers. Let the relaxation go even further, becoming more and more relaxed.

Now, turn your attention to your chest and stomach. As you inhale and exhale, there is a gentle rhythmic massaging action that loosens tight chest muscles and allows your abdomen and stomach to relax. Let it go further and further. Relax more and more. Feel the relaxation in your hips and buttocks as you rest comfortably, becoming more and more deeply relaxed. Continue letting go more and more. Now, sense the relaxation in your thighs and into the calves of both your legs, becoming more and more relaxed. Now, let the relaxation move down into your feet, further and more deeply relaxed. Now, one by one, think of individual body parts. As you think of each part, allow yourself to feel the relaxation becoming even deeper, part by part .... hands .... forearms .... upper arms ... shoulders ... neck ... jaws ... mouth ... tongue ... eyes ... buttocks ... thighs ... calves ... and toes. Feel the total relaxation throughout your body. A calm feeling develops and intensifies. Just continue to let go, just letting go more and more.

To help you relax even more, count slowly from ten to one. You may want to picture yourself going down a long flight of stairs or a long escalator into a place of deeper and deeper comfort and peace, perhaps a lush garden or a spot near a peaceful lake. *Choose a place that suggests deep peace and comfort to you. Refer to it here and during the countdown.*

As each number is said, see if you can let go and relax a little bit more. Even when it seems impossible to relax any further, there is always that extra bit of calm and relaxation that you can enjoy, simply by letting go more and more.

Ten . . . relaxing more and more
Seven . . . feel that relaxation all over
Six . . . even more comfortable
Five . . . halfway there, closer and closer to *your peaceful place*
Four . . . deeper and still further relaxed
Three . . . letting go even more
Two . . . still more relaxed
One . . . enjoy the relaxed feelings

Just continue relaxing for a while. When you are ready to stop, slowly stretch your body, breathe in and out deeply, and gradually get up and resume your normal activities. Continuing to feel calm and relaxed, yet wide awake and very alert.

The next exercise is a good one to try after a week or two of experience with one or more of the other methods. It is a very quick way to relax and starts the process of shortening the amount of time required to enter the receptive state you need to accomplish your goals.

**Script 4:**
**Rapid Relaxation**
*Time required: 3 to 4 minutes*
Once you are comfortable, take in a really deep breath. Completely fill your lungs. As you are breathing in, tense every muscle in your body. Hold your breath in, and study the tension in every part of your body. Now exhale allowing your entire body to relax. Feel the relief as the relaxation spreads all over and as you let go more and more. Do you know just how deeply relaxed you are? And do you know just how deeply relaxed you can be? Now breathe again, fill your lungs with air, and push your stomach out — hold it. Now let it out slowly. Continue to breathe normally — in and out. Now, as you breathe in, think the word *in*, and as you breathe out, think the word *out*. Let go of all your muscles so that you feel pleasantly heavy and calm, and each time you exhale, feel yourself breathing all the remaining tensions out of your body. Do you know just how much comfort you can feel? Now continue relaxing like that for as long as you'd like.

Now allow your mind to come up with a word or phrase that describes your present relaxed state. *Use your cue word or phrase here. If by chance you don't already have one, now's the time to come up with one.* Say your cue word each time you exhale for a moment or two. You should repeat your word or phrase whenever you feel this relaxed. The more you do this, the sooner that word or phrase will evoke these relaxed feelings whenever you desire.

When you are ready to stop, take a deep breath and open your eyes as you exhale. Feel awake, alert, and nicely relaxed. Remember to stretch your body before getting up, and then slowly stand up and resume your normal activities.

## Making Changes
In this last phase of programming the mind, I will share three different methods. These are recalling past successes, imagining results, and changing the structure of dreams.

## Recalling Past Successes
When embarking on a new venture in which you lack confidence, you should make accomplishing it your ultimate goal. Making the Dean's List or getting a promotion or anything reasonable may be the goal you chose.

First, relax using your cue word or the entire technique. Now, recall a past success such as being on the honor roll in high school or getting a particularly good grade on a difficult test. Imagine the pride and confidence you experienced when you did that. Now, using your short-range goals, look at the first one. Imagine yourself achieving this goal. If it is to study, make it a particular time of day and focus on that. Think about your ultimate goal. After coming out of your relaxation, work on putting that first step into practice. Do this for each item on your short-range goal list until you have accomplished your ultimate goal.

Here is an example of a relaxation technique specifically for recalling and using a past success for a present or future success (Mind Power p. 124).

**Imagining the Results**
In this type of technique you imagine already achieving the results
you want. First, regularly fantasize about what your life would be
like after you reach this goal. This will force you to think about
yourself in an entirely new light. This will give you a new identity
and self-perception. This is not to be confused with wishful thinking. Imagining enlists powerful resources of human imagination in
systematic and proven ways to achieve certain ends.

If your goal is being less depressed, you can structure a system to
facilitate its remission. In the case of a death, a mission statement might be that the lost loved one would want you to go on
with your life. Short-range goals could include eating at a regular
time, using relaxation to help you sleep, spending time with friends,
going to church, and so on. Using the relaxation technique, you
can imagine yourself not depressed and what your loved one
would be doing. You could imagine yourself as being confident, in
less pain, and anything else related to recovery. Another useful
idea is playing music in your head, which gives you a feeling of
strength and power, perhaps a gospel song or hymn.

**Changing Perspective & Structure of Imagery**
When using imagery, you can manipulate its strength and power.
If there is something you would like to accomplish, you will want
to be in the image. In my clinical work, the most frightening night
terrors are those in which the person dreaming is an active
participant in the dream. Being in a dream or nightmare is always
more powerful than dreaming as an observer. Use this knowledge
to your advantage. If you want to change something in your life,
do not make your dream like watching a movie but become an
actor in the movie. This can make your imagining more powerful.

If there is a condition or situation that gives you a problem
involving an in-law, boss, neighbor, or anything, use imagery to

make them smaller, make yourself larger, and/or take yourself out of the picture.

These techniques will make you the master of your own fate. God gave us dominion over all the earth and the gift of free will. It is our responsibility to use them to our fullest potential, as in the parable of the master who, prior to going on a long journey, gave three servants differing amounts of money. The first two servants increased their master's money and were rewarded. The third gave back what he was given and was admonished (Matthew 25:14, Luke 19:12-27). When you meet your master will you be rewarded or admonished?

# Relationships

In this part, I will discuss relationships — heterosexual, romantic relationships established for the purpose of having a good and lasting marriage.

The most wonderful experience we can have in this life and in the next is that of having love. I will draw on knowledge from Scripture, professional experiences as a family and couples therapist, and my own happy marriage. I will share the most important elements I have found pertinent to a happy marriage. This should by no means be construed as a substitute for psychotherapy if a relationship is in trouble, but as adjunct information.

My original purpose for compiling this information was to inform my teenage daughter about the basics of relationships. Choosing a mate is one of the most important choices we will make. It can be the best thing that can happen or the worst thing you've ever done. It is seldom in between. The problem is no one ever talks about how to go about choosing a mate. It is much better to get it right the first time than to go through the misery, heartache, and legal fees associated with separation or divorce. Because the decision to marry is too important to leave to chance, attraction and/or lust, I put this information together to tell my daughter what to look for in a mate. If you do not have a standard for a mate, you are at risk of accepting anything that comes along. As those of us who are older know, not all that glitters is gold.

## Marriage
God created the first marriage when He created Eve. God planned for Adam and Eve to remain together in love, peace, and harmony for eternity. However, because of their disobedience, difficulties

were placed in their relationship. We are all familiar with their disobedience but may be less clear about the specifics of God's curse. "And He said to the woman. I will increase your trouble in pregnancy and your pain in giving birth. In spite of this, you will still have desire for your husband, yet you will be subject to him" (Genesis 3:16). If you cannot accept these conditions for marriage you need to remain single.

Since that time man has complicated the situation. During the time of Exodus the Israelites wanted a method by which they could divorce or put away their mates. Moses reluctantly decreed that a man could put away his wife if she were adulterous. This was the only accepted reason for separation or divorce (Exodus 21:7-11). Even with this law, Jesus taught that there was no acceptable reason for divorce (Mark 10:2-12). With this in mind, it becomes very important to choose the right mate, the first time. In discussing relationships with my daughter, I started with common-sense basics.

When my daughter was about 14 and became interested in dating, the first thing I told her was, "If you want to know where a boy is coming from, look at what he does. Does he keep his word? Is he a hot head? Does he use drugs? Does he work?" "Even a child shows what he is by what he does; you can tell if he is honest and good," (Proverbs 20:11). You learn much more about a person by what they do rather than just what they say. This was specifically aimed at her not being pressured into having sexual intercourse. The second thing I told her was to look at the quality of the boy's relationship with his mother. It is not likely a man will ever respect any woman more than he respects his mother. This information did her well until she left home to attend college. When my daughter was about 19 and a college student, relationships took on a more serious tone. At that point, I felt she was ready for "Relationships 202" or more advanced information about relationships.

I told her that there are different types of relationships. After all,

I felt it would be unlikely that her first relationship would be with her future husband. In contemplating relationships, one can consider the quality of relationships along various lines. One such way is to consider two types of relationships. (Two categories of romantic relationships may sound simplistic, but simple is good complex is human.) God had 10 Commandments; Jesus reduced them to one, love. Jesus also said, *"You cannot serve God and man,"* (Matthew 6:24). We must choose one. There is good and evil, no third choice. In the spirit of simplicity, I offer two descriptions of relationships: 1) the Short-term, Recreational/Disposable Relationship and 2) the Long-term 50-Year Marriage Relationship.

### Short-term Relationships

A short-term, disposable relationship is based on tangible and superficial qualities such as, sexiness, party person, handsomeness, beauty, good dresser, status, money, and the like. Short-term relationships are built on personality. Personality is what you use to manipulate others for your own gain. Here, an individual will do whatever it takes to influence another or to get what he wants. Charm and pseudo-interest in another's interests and hobbies are used as techniques of human relations. Short-term relationships are not a bad thing in and of themselves as long as they are not used as substitutes for a long-term marriage relationship.

Short-term relationships often serve useful purposes. They can be fun and adventurous learning experiences. Sometimes, they serve the purpose of relieving loneliness. It is good to have a special someone who can pick you up when you're down, listen to your problems, teach you about yourself and the other sex. In my own life, I found that during the period prior to meeting my mate, I learned a lot about women from women, such as what they like, do not like, and expect from a man. These valuable lessons were best learned before I married. At that time, many of my best friends were women. It was a girlfriend that first told me I was intelligent and encouraged me to go to college. Women were my first confidants. They helped me learn things about myself. However nice, beautiful, or intelligent these women were, none was destined to be my wife but all contributed to my having a successful marriage. They taught me the value of patience, sensitivity, loyalty, and much more. Most of all, they taught me that making love is more than sex.

Short-term relationships have no terms presented by the man and accepted by the woman. These relationships are disposable. It is a waste of time, effort, and love to fix a short-term relationship when it goes bad. When it goes bad, take what you can, like lessons learned, and move on.

## Long-term Relationships
Long-term relationships are built on character and terms. Character is a primary trait. Personality is a secondary trait. Character is who we are. With character, long-term relationships are based on integrity, humility, fidelity, temperance, courage, justice, patience, industry, and everything else in God's definition of love. The character ethic is based on principles that govern behavior. This is very much like the law of behavior found in the Ten Commandments. Like Cecil B. DeMille said, "We cannot break the Law. We can only break ourselves if we violate the Law." If you want to know what kind of character lies beneath the personality, watch what a person does in a crisis. The problems of life will strip away personality. What you will see then is the person's character.

In establishing a long-term 50-year marriage relationship, there must be terms on which the relationship will be based. That is, the man has to present terms upon which he bases his life and intends to base his marriage. The terms might include how the home is to be run, what is acceptable, his responsibilities, and what his expectations are for his wife and children. Remember, one of the curses Adam and Eve passed on to us was the Scriptural directive that the woman is subject to the man (Genesis 3:16). This is what makes the man the head of the household. What this does not mean is that the man is the king, dictator, or perhaps master. It means it is up to the man to establish family direction. An example of this can be where it is said; "As for me and my house, we will worship the Lord," (Joshua 24:15).

In our patriarchal western culture, it is customary for a man to propose to a woman. It is the woman's prerogative to accept or reject his proposal. Let's look at what a proposal is more closely. It is more than a man asking a woman to marry him. A proposal is an offer of terms for which a product will be delivered. This is true of any proposal, whether it is for medical work, electrical work, or any type of contract or covenant. As such, a long-term 50-year marriage relationship is based on terms that the man presents. Beauty, stature, money, class, station in life, and the like should become secondary. These may have been primary in the short-term relationship and a factor in attracting two people together for consideration of a long-term relationship but are not as important in the long-term relationship itself.

In my own relationship we had a crisis when it was time to present my terms. Because I had been somewhat promiscuous in the early phase of our relationship, before we married, Maxine said, "Earle, if you fool around, I'm going to mess around too." I'm not sure if she really meant it or if she just used this tactic to see what I would do, but it forced me to put my terms on the table. I said, "Honey, if you want to mess around, don't wait for me. That is your body to do with what you want. But I'll tell you what, if you are true to your God and I'm true to my God, we will automatically be true to each other. "My belief in Christianity forced me to choose the direction our relationship would take. Additionally, I read in Scripture that adultery and fornication are the only sins mentioned that we commit against ourselves. My terms then, were not that I was asking Maxine to be true to me, or for me to be true to her, but that we would use our Christian faith to be true to our God. My fidelity or infidelity is not her problem. My infidelity would be my problem. This would be a problem between God and me. Consequently, we have not had to deal with this issue since then.

When I proposed to Maxine, I had other terms as well, such as no violence, cursing, or arguing, to name a few. This was how I wanted my home to operate. For me, my home is a place to recharge my batteries and rest so I can deal effectively with the world. These were my terms. It was up to Maxine to accept or reject them. I am a blessed man for her acceptance of my terms.

Even when terms have been established, if the man reneges on his own terms, it can cause a crisis in the relationship. The nature of the crisis can cause a leadership vacuum. Because a vacuum cannot be tolerated and a marriage cannot be leaderless, the wife will invariably be forced to assume leadership. In my professional experience, the reneging of terms usually results in three things: the man feeling castrated, an increase in arguments, and an increase in conflicts. This type of marriage, where the husband allows his place as head of the household to be usurped, will invariably foster hostility. For the relationship to endure, the husband needs to reclaim his place as the head of the house by reinstating the original terms or renegotiating new ones. If he does not, the relationship will not endure because the wife no longer needs him and may no longer respect him.

Even without a betrayal of terms and with character, other obstacles can impede a 50-year marriage. Relationships may need to be adjusted from time to time, pretty much like a tune up. The couple needs to fix it, hire a mechanic like a therapist, attend a marriage encounter group, or the like.

People get into trouble when they mistake a short-term relationship for a long-term, 50-year, marriage relationship. If I had to reduce criteria for distinguishing a short- term relationship from a marriage relationship to two aspects, I would say terms and character. If there is something major you would like to change in your mate, he or she is possibly not the person to marry.

## What Love Is and Is Not

One of the sticking points of marriage is what happens after the honeymoon. Dr. Peck, in his book <u>A Road Less Traveled,</u> points out that loving does not start until after one falls out of love. Because this may sound like a paradox, let me explain.

According to Dr. Peck, falling in love is like a psychological brainwashing of lust. This physiological phenomenon is designed to attract men and women together for the purpose of procreation and the continuation of the species. We cannot force the process of falling in love. It is automatic and instinctual. Because we do not exert effort to experience this feeling, we do not really deserve credit for its occurrence.

After we have fallen in love, or chosen to be in love, and decided that a particular person fulfills the requirements for a 50-year marriage relationship, we marry. We may find that after the honeymoon, we are falling out of love. This is natural as we begin to see the forest full of trees. We now realize our mate is not perfect, not our clone, not the most brilliant, clever, pretty, or handsome person on the planet. You are now in the process of removing the facade you have superimposed on your mate and now see him/her for who they really are. You are falling out of love.

Many people get stuck here in this phase of marriage where the couple is likely to engage in fights, quarrels, adultery, or self-destructive behaviors. These behaviors can include violence, drugs, alcohol, or work-a-holism. However, those in successful long-term relationships know that there is a way out. They become loving. This is the work of marriage. Loving, unlike falling in love, requires effort. Being loving, according to Dr. Peck, involves the work of investing time and energy into another for their own and their mate's personal growth and development. The real work is to be loving even when you do not feel like it. Falling in love gets you to the altar or justice of the peace. Being loving gets you to your 50th wedding anniversary. As you learn to do this, you will find that the love you end up with will be better, much better, than the love with which you began.

Many think love is a consumer activity or spectator sport. It is neither. Love is the accurate estimate and supply of another's need. Meeting and supplying another's needs should not be confused with assuming responsibility for another's happiness. Each of us is responsible for our own happiness. You bring your own happiness to the relationship. Symbolically speaking, it is like each of us bringing our own cake to the relationship. The best your mate can do is to add to your happiness or put frosting on your cake. Bring your own cake. We cannot be expected to supply our mate's basic happiness. However, if each mate tries to spoil the other, your mate will have plenty of frosting. Acting as only a consumer of love will drain and deplete your mate. Acting as both a supplier and consumer will keep both of you happier. Love as a verb is longer lasting than love as a noun. In other words, love is an action. It is something you do.

"God is the essence of love," (1 John 4:6). His Word gives us an in-depth description of how genuine love expresses itself. First Corinthians 13, commonly called the Love Chapter, spells out the real meaning of love. Lust doesn't measure up to this interpretation; in fact it violates it. Let's compare God's assessment of love to the devil's counterfeit — lust.

## Love (Long-term 50-Year Marriage Relationship)
1. Love is patient.
2. Love is kind.
3. Love does not envy.
4. Love does not boast.
5. Love is not rude.
6. Love is not self-seeking.
7. Love is not easily angered.
8. Love does not keep a record of wrongs.
9. Love does not delight in evil.
10. Love is not proud.
11. Love rejoices in truth.
12. Love always protects.
13. Love always trusts.
14. Love always hopes.
15. Love always preserves.
16. Love never fails; is constant, enduring, and faithful to the end.

## Lust (Short-term Recreational Relationship)
1. Lust can't wait, is impulsive.
2. Lust is cruel, critical, and manipulative.
3. Lust seeks more than it earns.
4. Lust builds self at another's expense.
5. Lust is easily threatened.
6. Lust is disrespectful and thoughtless.
7. Lust is demanding and uncaring.
8. Lust is temperamental and restless.
9. Lust does not forget offenses.
10. Lust commits wrongs to get its own way, rationalizes.
11. Lust encourages lies and covers up mistakes/misdeeds.
12. Lust takes to gain its own ends; lacks concern for consequences to others.
13. Lust is suspicious and jealous.
14. Lust says one chance and you're out.

15. Lust backs out when it is no longer convenient.
16. Lust ceases when self is no longer served. It is fickle insecure, and unfaithful.

This is what you get when you try to make a 50-year marriage out of a short-term relationship. In my professional and social experience it seems that the reason this happens is because both or one of the participants is in love with love. That is, they are in love with the idea of being in love, not the actual person they are dealing with. There is a song whose lyrics sums up this concept succinctly, "Love Don't Love Nobody".

Lust can be addictive and difficult to release. In a situation such as this, it is better to do what is good for you rather than what feels good. Feelings can lie. Lust, like illegal drugs, can feel good and be addictive but in your mind and soul, you know what is not good for you and what is good for you. If you are still confused, ask someone you trust. Be careful.

It is also important to realize that relationships are not always 50/50 propositions. There will be times in the relationship when one will give 70% and the other 30%. As long as the giving and taking are complementary, both will grow. If you keep your expectations low, you will appreciate each other's contributions as a bonus.

## Scriptural Characteristics of the Ideal Mate

Now that we have discussed various components/concepts of relationships and God's definition of love verses Satan's counterfeit of lust, the question becomes who is the right woman or man for me? What does he or she look like? How will I know when the right one comes along? Of course the other question might be what characteristics do I need to possess in order to qualify for an ideal mate? We find descriptions of the "Capable Wife" in Proverbs 31:10-31.

First we will examine how Scripture describes a good woman. After all, we would want to be able to recognize her should she come our way. I truly believe we attract people that are like ourselves. The old saying "birds of a feather flock together" has real merit. It means if you want to know what type of person you are, look at your friends. Chances are they are just like you. Applied to the topic of choosing the right mate, if you find yourself attracted to the same type of mate you do not want over and over again, look at yourself. To find the capable mate, you have to be a capable mate. Scripture says a good wife is a blessing from the Lord. To get a blessing, you have to be a blessing. While what is described here sounds like perfection, it is a good model to which we can aspire.

## The Capable Wife

As I share this Scripture from Proverbs 31:10-31 I would like you to interpret what the passage means to you:

1. *How hard it is to find a capable wife! She is worth far more than jewels! Her husband puts his confidence in her, and he will never be poor.*

2. *As long as she lives, she does him good and never harm.*

3. *She keeps herself busy making wool and linen cloth.*

4. *She brings him food from out of the way places, as merchant ships do.*

5. *She gets up before daylight to prepare food for her family and tells her servant girls what to do.*

6. *She looks at land and buys it, and with money she has earned plants a vineyard.*

7. *She is a hard worker, strong, and industrious.*

8. *She knows the value of everything she makes and works late into the night.*

9.  She spins her own thread and weaves her own clothes.

10. She is generous to the poor and needy.

11. She doesn't worry when it snows because her family has warm clothing.

12. She makes bedspreads and wears clothes of fine linen.

13. Her husband is well known, one of the leading citizens.

14. She makes clothes and belts.

15. She is strong and respected and not afraid of the future.

16. She speaks with a gentle wisdom.

17. She is always busy and looks after her family's needs.

18. Her children show their appreciation, and her husband praises her.

Also included in Proverbs is advice on how to keep a good wife. "Find a wife and you find a good thing; it shows the Lord is good to you" (Proverbs 18:22). You see a man can build a house but it takes a good wife to make it a home. Consider Proverbs 14:1 where it says; "Homes are made by the wisdom of women, but are destroyed by foolishness." So fellas, don't be foolish. Husbands need to tell their wives, "Many women are good wives, but you are the best of all," (Proverbs 31:29) and "Charm is deceptive and beauty disappears, but a woman who honors the Lord should be praised," (Proverbs 31:30). Remember, charm and beauty are the traits of short-term relationships.

Of course there are behaviors a good wife will want to avoid such as, "A nagging wife is like water going drip-drip-drip" (Proverbs 19:13) or "Better to live on a roof than share the house with a nagging wife," (Proverbs 21:9).

## The Capable Husband
Descriptions of good men found in Scripture are not as well packaged as they are for a good wife, but they are there through-

out the Scriptures: "*If you are sensible you will control your temper,*" (Ephesians 4:26), "*When someone wrongs you, it is great virtue to ignore it,*" (Proverbs 19:11), "*A good man's words are a fountain of life*" (Proverbs 10:11), "*A good man's words will benefit many people,*" (Proverbs 10:21) and "*A good man's words are like pure silver,*" (Proverbs 10:20). Here are 10 other traits of a good man (married or unmarried) I would like to share with you:

1. *The man who puts God's business above any of his own affairs* (Romans 14:8)

2. *The man who teaches and sets a good example for his children* (Deuteronomy 6:6,7)

3. *The man who recognizes that anyone who needs him is his neighbor* (Luke 10:27,29,33)

4. *The man who measures his giving by what he has left rather than by what he gives* (II Corinthians 9:6)

5. *The man who reads the Word of God with as much diligence as he does the daily paper* (II Timothy 2:15)

6. *The man who lives for the treasures in heaven rather than the pleasures on earth* (Matthew 6:20,21)

7. *The man who recognizes his obligations to his family, his church, and his community as well as to his business* (Luke 12:19,20)

8. *The man who sees his own faults before he sees the faults of others* (Matthew 7:3)

9. *The man who wants to help others rather than serve himself* (Philippians 2:3,4)

10. *The man who recognizes that all of life should be lived distinctively* (I Corinthians 10:31)

Understand that these are suggestions of what an ideal wife and husband should look like according to Scripture. If these traits do not describe you, then perhaps these can be personal and spiritual goals. It may be time to re-create yourself.

So far, we have described types of relationships as short-term recreational or long-term 50-year marriage. We have explored what love is and is not, what to do when the honeymoon is over, and Scriptural characteristics of a good wife and good husband. We will now explore interpersonal and intrapersonal intimacy skills from a psychological perspective.

## Interpersonal Skills

Interpersonal skills are the traits and actions that you use when relating to other people. They include the following abilities and beliefs:

1. Compassion- the ability to identify with the needs of another.

2. Caring presence- the ability to listen actively.

3. Generosity- approachability and availability and the sharing of one's resources, abilities, and time.

4. Being "other centered"- starting with needs of others rather than one's own needs.

5. Confiding- opening up one's self for purposes of growth.

6. Trust- the belief the other will understand us.

7. Loyalty- commitment to the unit that surpasses the self.

8. Expression of affection- tactile expressions of love such as holding, touching, kissing, etc.

9. Inclusive relationship- the ability to invite your mate in.

10. Commitment- a life-long commitment to the other.

11. Skills for fidelity- the ability to be faithful.

### Intrapersonal Skills

Intrapersonal skills are the traits and actions that you use when relating to yourself. These include:

1. Self-esteem development- the reverence of self as a gift from God.

2. Enjoyment of one's own company- the ability to be alone without being lonely.

3. Internal locus of control- the ability to look into self as the cause of the good and bad that happens to self.

4. Appreciating God as the grounding of one's life- a relationship of joyful integrity in the love of God.

5. Appreciating one's own sexuality- grateful for one's sexuality, geniality, attraction, and arousal mechanism.

6. Awareness of gratitude in one's life- blessing another with expressions of gratitude.

These are suggestions, for skills once mastered and practiced which will not only help us become better mates but better people as well.

# How to Keep a Good Thing Going

One of the biggest complaints I hear in couples therapy deals with communication, that is, effective communication. It is not that the couple does not know how to communicate because if they did not, they never would have been able to marry in the first place. By effective communication, I am referring to the meaningful exchange of ideas, feelings, and opinions in a respectful and civil manner. This is about talking; more importantly, it is about listening. It is not about complaining, arguing, and threatening.

Once, while doing couple's therapy, a husband remarked that

everyone argues. I thought for a moment, and said, my wife and I do not argue. When I went home that night, I asked my wife about this. She said, "Well, I think we had an argument in 1986 but I'm not sure." This was in 1997. Arguing is not a normal part of a relationship, unless you want it to be. Sure, there are times I may want to argue, and I get angry, but I do not act on it. We can have differences of opinion and if we cannot resolve it, we agree to disagree. It is not always easy, but it is possible.

Only good communication will facilitate a happy, growth-producing, 50-year marriage. Bad communication which I find in troubled relationships is either destructive or not understood. By this, I mean the use of drugs, infidelity, violence, and the like accompany this type of relationship. All of these actions communicate dissatisfaction with domestic issues and can destroy the relationship or at best leave your mate without a way to respond or understand.

In order to improve communication, what I suggest is two-fold: First, Scripture points out, *"Do not let the sun set on your anger, nor give place to the Devil,"* (Ephesians 4:26). Do not go to sleep angry. Related to this is my belief that everything we do in life pleases someone, in the spiritual realm, either God or the Devil. Whomever we serve on earth is our master. Because we will spend eternity with our master, it is wise to choose our master well.

Evil forces are committed to the destruction of your marriage, which God has put together. When you are angry with your mate, demons will whisper things in your ear to remind you of past hurts you thought you had forgotten. You may become lustful or keep a record of wrongs. These thoughts will help you rationalize and intellectualize negative behavior. They might say things like, "You should leave him/her", or "You should hurt him/her," or "This other person shows you more love and respect than your mate," or something similar. Psychologists call this self-talk. Demons use the psychology of suggestion, rationalization, and intellectualization against you.

Second, never discuss a controversy with your mate while angry. This is a technique often suggested by mental health professionals when teaching parenting skills. It is said that parents should not punish their children while angry. An adaptation of this technique is useful in marriage. That is, wait until you have calmed down before presenting your side of the controversy. Do not disagree with each other while angry. A good rule of thumb is found in standard conflict resolution/negotiation techniques, a technique also used by therapists. This technique involves validating the other person's point of view before presenting your own. For instance, you come home late at night and have missed the supper your mate prepared. He/she starts fussing at you. Your conflict resolution response might sound something like this; "I can understand why you are upset. We were looking forward to this time together and you are hurt and angry. You put a lot of effort in this meal but honey on my way home..." In this way you defuse a potential argument. Your mate feels validated and is in a better position to hear your excuse. Also related to this intervention is the ability to compromise. Understand you will not always get your own way completely, all the time. If compromise is not possible and negotiation skills are ineffective, your last resort may be to agree to disagree. Just because the two of you are mates, it is not necessary or reasonable to expect to agree on everything.

In the book, <u>Men Are From Mars, Women Are From Venus</u>, the author, John Gray, Ph.D., presents a point of view that appears useful. In it, he explains that when a man has a problem and talks about it, he is primarily looking for a solution. However, when a woman has a problem, she is not necessarily looking for a solution but just wants to be heard, understood, and appreciated. Where a man wants a solution, a woman may prefer empathy.

Someone once said that men are less complicated than women. All a man needs is a good wife and a hobby to occupy his time. Women are much more complicated and better at managing a relationship. Think about this for a minute. The language of a man is action; for a woman it is words. There may be some truth to this when you consider what each gender likes to do and observe.

Typically, men like sports. They like action that is direct, uncomplicated, and measurable. Women, however, tend to like movies that involve indirect communication and complex relationships. This is the type of material found in soap operas and romantic movies. This is not an effort to stereotype men and women but just a way of trying to understand their differences. Most men could care less about who is sleeping with whom. Most women could care less about who will win the playoffs. If this makes any sense, then it is probably better to let the woman run the relationship and let the man have his hobby.

Love has a language of its own. Here are my 5 languages of love:

1. **Spoiling Your Mate.** The idea of spoiling a person is often given a negative connotation but I think it can be a good thing if mates try to spoil each other. One of the best ways to spoil your mate and make him/her feel loved is to give compliments.

2. **Gratitude.** It is good to be grateful. Thank your wife for cleaning and cooking. There really is nothing that says she has to do it. Thank your husband for all the chores he does around the house, working, and other things he does.

3. **Appreciation.** Do not take your wife or husband for granted. Ego stroking for a man and a woman goes a long way. A wife

who can tell her husband that he is handsome makes him feel good. If he feels like a king, he is more likely to treat his wife like a queen. If a man treats his wife like a queen, she is more likely to treat him like a king.

4. **Together Activities.** Another general category of things that help a relationship grow is doing things together. It is good to work, play, and pray together.

5. **Tactile Stimulation.** Another important thing to do is to sleep together. This is more than having sex with each other. Touching and holding each other can be just as effective and intimate as intercourse.

## Sexual Intercourse

No conversation about relationships would be complete without mentioning sex. Sex is very possibly the best physical feeling one can experience. Sexual intercourse is an important part of the human experience that God created to ensure procreation. Sex is mentioned quite often in Scripture. As a matter of fact, sex is such a good feeling that even angels like to do it. *"Some of the heavenly beings saw that these girls were beautiful, so they took the ones they liked. Then the Lord said, 'I will not allow people to live forever, they are mortal. From now on they will live no longer than 120 years'. In those days and even later, there were giants on the earth who were descendants of human women and the heavenly beings. They were great heroes and famous men of long ago"* (Genesis 6:2-4). The Song of Solomon was about this king's love, relationship, and intimacy. The New Testament contains a verse that says, *"if you cannot refrain from having sex, let each man/woman have his/her own mate,"* (I Corinthians 7:9).

Sex is generally a good barometer of the status of a relationship. One of the first questions I ask when doing couples therapy is, "How's the sex?" Any changes in the frequency or intensity of intercourse is cause for concern. When either partner feels unloved, intercourse is lessened or eliminated. Then there is the risk of an extra-marital affair or other behavior to fill the void such as using drugs, staying out late at night, becoming a work-a-holic, or engaging in some other activity to sublimate libidinal energy.

## Interventions

I am going to try to explain interventions I know and use in treatment, and I would like to share the most salient ones I use in treatment with clients. The first thing I tell clients is that treatment with me does not involve looking for someone to blame. My treatment is entirely solution focused. That is, what is it going to take to get the relationship back on track?

Clearly, the most powerful intervention I have used can be reduced to one word, forgiveness. Psychologists and other mental health professionals used to be taught that when confronted with an angry client, we should allow them to vent their hostilities. Venting is not only ineffective; it can also be spiritually dangerous. Venting may only serve the purpose of feeding your demon. Scripture says, "Let not the sun set on your anger, nor give place to the Devil," (Ephesians 4:26). If you feed your demon, you make him stronger. You might say, "Well, doctor, if venting anger is not the solution, what is?" Glad you asked. Forgiveness is the solution — just as Christ who died on the cross forgave His tormentors, just as Christ forgave Peter when he denied him three times, and just as Christ forgave the apostles when they could not stay awake long enough to pray with Him in the garden of Gethsemane. Forgiveness is the resolution to anger and can be applied to any and all situations of anger, whether or not my client is a Christian.

In a treatment situation where the man or woman has been unfaithful, the ability to forgive has surmounted pride, anger, and sense of betrayal. Often, however, there are often serious impediments blocking the victim's ability to forgive. It is a very difficult thing to do and is mentioned in Scripture. "But a man who commits adultery doesn't have good sense..." (Proverbs 6:32). "A husband is never angrier than when he is jealous; his revenge knows no limits," (Proverbs 6:34). "He will not accept any payment; no amount of gifts will satisfy his anger," (Proverbs 6:35). However, I have treated couples where the wife has cheated and couples where the husband has cheated. In both situations, they were able to keep the relationship together and in some cases, become stronger and better.

Forgiveness is perhaps the most profound expression of love. And love is always more powerful than hate. Why? Because God is love. Hate is demonic, and God is more powerful than Satan. Forgiveness is the forerunner of peace of mind and acceptance. This act of forgiveness is portrayed over and over again in Scripture (Matthew 6:14-15, 9:2, Luke 17:3). "And how many times shall I forgive my brother, seven times?" Christ was asked. Jesus replied 70 times 7 (Matthew 18:21-35). We can take this to mean infinity. Of course there are conditions attached just as there are conditions attached to God forgiving our sins, that is, we must be sincere and resolve not to do it again.

When Christ forgave Peter his denial of Him, Christ asked Peter if he loved Him three times after His resurrection. When the apostles fell asleep Christ said, "The spirit is willing but the flesh is weak" (Matthew 26:41). When Christ forgave the good thief there was in his case as in the others I just mentioned, an act of contrition or resolution to not sin this sin again.

I bring this up because our flesh is probably no stronger than the apostles or the Good Thief. As such, we will all make mistakes. Human nature is like that. It's about turning the other cheek. While forgiveness does not always make human sense, it always makes divine sense. Human nature wants revenge, "an eye for an eye". But Jesus came to fulfill the law.

In therapy, I find that the biggest stumbling block a person encounters is forgiving their mate for some past unresolved hurt. Evil forces will remind you of past pain that you thought you forgot. Forgiveness and patience will always be the most powerful glue to hold a family together.

Another therapy technique used successfully is improved communication. I am specifically talking about good communication, described earlier. This can be verbal or behavioral. A verbal intervention I use is that of a couple picking a specific time of day to do this exercise. They are to sit face to face while one begins to talk for 5 minutes, without interruption. The mate then repeats what he or she has heard and then responds. Then this mate takes a turn speaking and the other listens and responds. Practicing this exercise promotes listening skills. The couple is instructed to take turns going first, use a stopwatch, to do this for one week, and assess the results.

Sometimes, couples don't know how to talk to each other but are full of love. In this case, I suggest that they buy a card that expresses a sentiment or message they want to convey to their spouse. After exchanging cards, I ask them individually what their card said. Usually, they have not looked at the card they sent after giving it to their mate. By asking them to recall the message it begins to teach them how to talk to each other and to pay attention. A spontaneous card or gift adds an element of adventure to a relationship that can rekindle flames of love. Understand you cannot put a relationship on automatic pilot and think it will fly by itself. Relationships need to be nourished and stirred up from time to time, or they will get stale, boring, and ripe for temptation.

Once I had a client, a retired military man, who was court ordered for treatment due to his conviction of shoplifting. As it turned out, he was a kleptomaniac. After he had been in treatment for about 6 weeks, we were able to bring his kleptomania under control with the behavioral technique of thought stopping. Thought stopping is a technique where the client is instructed to wear an elastic band on his wrist. Whenever an unwanted thought or impulse comes up, he/she is instructed to snap the elastic on the inside of the wrist. This really stings and will usually take your mind off the unwanted thought. Eventually, you learn to substitute a positive thought or Scriptural truth in place of the elastic and thereby control unwanted thoughts and impulses. The next phase of treatment called for the use of insight-oriented psychotherapy to find the origins of this man's behavior. This client was not a criminal type. He had never stolen anything prior to this phase of his life. He was now stealing things he could afford to pay for and for which he had no use. As a Christian Psychologist, I believe everything happens for a reason. After all God created a universe that is orderly. There is a reason for everything.

In looking for the root of the problem, I discovered that my client's stealing started shortly after he and his wife started drifting apart and stopped having sexual intercourse. This had gone on for over a year. He had forgotten how to talk to his wife and both were suffering in silence. Both felt rejected. I had both of them exchange cards for two weeks and read the cards to each other. Soon after, they began having sex and fell in love, all over again. As I said earlier, the frequency and intensity of sexual intercourse is always a good barometer of the state of the rela-tionship. I am convinced that most, if not all-emotional distress has its roots in the perception of not being loved. In this case, the man's kleptomania stopped. He was cured.

Earlier, I mentioned pride as another barrier to forgiveness. But first, I have a riddle. What is the first thing you should do when you find yourself in a rut? Answer: put the shovel down. When your relationship is going badly you make it worse (dig deeper) with pride, anger, drug use, or violence. These become shovels that make your rut deeper and therefore more difficult to get out of.

Johnny, a very wise older gentleman, gave sage advice to a friend. It seems a man, who loved his wife very much, decided to get a second job to bring home more money. His very beautiful wife soon became bored and lonely because her husband was not around. Eventually, she had an affair and was caught. The husband told this story to his wise old friend. Johnny advised the man not to tell this story to anyone else, not his friends or relatives, to see if the relationship could be repaired. The husband took this advice. His marriage grew stronger than it was before because he forgave his wife and she repented. The point is this. If the husband had told other people about his wife's affair, they may have encouraged him to leave her. At this point the husband's pride would have gotten in the way of his ability to forgive his wife. Marriage needs to be seen as a unit. In this arithmetic equation, 1 + 1 = more than 2. The unit is more important than either the husband or wife.

## Conclusion

We have discussed many aspects of relationships and marriage. We touched on different types of relationships, how to choose a mate, what a capable mate looks like, how to speak the language of love, and how to repair a broken marriage. I tell clients that you cannot give what you do not have. In other words, you cannot give me love if you do not love yourself, you cannot give me respect if you do not respect yourself, and so forth. Here are some questions to consider:

1. What do you want from a relationship?
2. What is it you do not want?
3. What should your relationship look like?

4. Would you marry just to get something you can buy i.e. cooking, sex, etc.?

5. Do you know someone in a successful marriage you can talk to before you marry?

6. Did you pray on your decision?

7. What do you want your home to be?

# Spiritual Relaxation

This is a relaxation technique that combines Christianity and Psychology. My purpose is to teach you about prayer and relaxation so you too may experience the peace of Christ. There are three things you must know and believe:

**God Speaks to Us First.** This fundamental truth makes it possible for us to pray to God. He has loved us long before we loved Him.

**God Wants to Communicate with Us**. God is speaking to us, continually revealing Himself to us through:
- Jesus Christ
- His word, the Bible
- the church, an extension of Christ in the world
- the events of our lives
- the Holy Spirit

**God Invites Us to Listen.** Our response to God's initial move should be to listen to what He is saying. This is the basic attitude of prayer.

## How to Listen

What we do prior to prayer is important. Prayer is not something to be rushed into. First you need to quiet yourself, relax, and settle into a prayerful and comfortable position. Try to find a quiet place where you can be alone and uninhibited in your response to God's presence. Jesus would often go up to a mountain by Himself to pray to His father. The following relaxation technique will help you be still. It is my experience that as Christians we are good at bringing our problems to the Lord, but we do not do well with leaving them with God. Therefore this relaxation method will also help you take your problems to God and leave them there.

## Relaxation Technique

I am going to share a relaxation technique with you in the form of directives, using visualizations. This has multiple purposes. It quiets anxiety, relieves stress, and puts you in a prayerful mood. You are then in a better position to hear God's message and His answers to your prayers.

This process will take about 20 minutes. If practiced daily, for about a month, it will allow you to go into a relaxed state by associating this process with a key word. Your key word can be anything such as, peace, calm, Christ, etc. The first couple of times you do it, you may fall asleep. After a while you will become accustomed to it. This process is entirely under your control. It is not hypnosis. You only need to relax as much as you would like. This process is most effective if read by another or tape-recorded.

### Relaxation Script

Open your eyes as wide as you can. Now slowly close your eyes. *Imagine Yourself Relaxing.*

Become aware of the point of maximum contact between your back and the back of your chair . . . *Imagine Yourself Relaxing*

Imagine that you are looking at something that is very far away . . . *Imagine Yourself Relaxing*

Feel the corners of your lips touching . . . *Imagine Yourself Relaxing*

Imagine one of God's most beautiful creations, a flower, suspended a few feet in front of you . . . *Imagine Yourself Relaxing*

Feel the gentlest breeze against your cheek . . . *Imagine Yourself Relaxing*

Be aware of one of your arms being heavier than the other . . . *Imagine Yourself Relaxing*

Be aware of one of your arms being lighter than the other . . . *Imagine Yourself Relaxing*

Feel the weight of your shoes on your feet . . . *Imagine Yourself Relaxing*

Imagine a leaf drifting slowly to the ground . . . *Imagine Yourself Relaxing*

Experience God's wonder of winter and the pristine freshness of freshly fallen snow. As you walk, the only sound you hear is the soft crunch of new snow under your feet . . . *Imagine Yourself Relaxing*

Experience God's wonder of spring where He makes all things new. Smell the delicate fragrances of colorful flowers . . . *Imagine Yourself Relaxing*

Experience God's wonder of summer. Feel the warmth of the high risen sun and hear the waves of the ocean lapping gently against the shore as you walk along the beach . . . *Imagine Yourself Relaxing*

Experience God's wonder of fall. See His multicolored creation in the leaves of the trees. Smell the fresh crisp air . . . *Imagine Yourself Relaxing*

Focus on your breath, as it becomes more and more shallow . . . *Imagine Yourself Relaxing*

Focus on your heart, as it becomes quieter and quieter . . . *Imagine Yourself Relaxing*

Now, focus on your pain, anguish, and heartache . . . *Imagine Yourself Relaxing*

Imagine you are approaching the throne of God . . . *Imagine Yourself Relaxing*

Now imagine all your pain drifting down your body from your head to your toes. Feel the tension leaving your forehead . . . your face eyes . . nose . . . cheeks . . . jaw . . . your neck . . . your shoulders . . . your back . . . your chest . . . your upper arms . . . your elbows . . . your forearm. . . your wrist . . . your hands . . . your fingers . . . your stomach . . . your hips . . . your groin . . . your thighs . . . your knees . . . your calves . . . your ankles . . . your feet . . . and finally your toes. All of your pain in the form of tension is draining down your body and out of your feet as you give God your problems . . . *Imagine Yourself Relaxing*

Forgive all those who have in any way caused you pain . . . *Imagine Yourself Relaxing*

Now that you have emptied yourself of pain and tension imagine the grace of God, as a beam of pure love from His heart to your heart, fill the void . . . *Imagine Yourself Relaxing*

Feel the comfort of God's peace and love, Father, Son, and Holy Spirit . . . *Imagine Yourself Relaxing*

Feel the strength of God flowing through you, around you, under you, over you, comforting you, loving you, and protecting you . . . *Imagine Yourself Relaxing*

As you leave the throne of God, feel His peace within you, always present, a permanent part of you. Just as exercising any physical muscle makes it bigger and stronger, feel your spiritual muscles growing bigger and stronger as a result of all the torment you have experienced. You are a spiritual giant because of Christ in you. And this strength will persist . . . *Imagine Yourself Relaxing*

As I count from 5 to 1, I want you to become more and more aware of your environment. More and more able to use the muscles of your body.

5 . . . you can move your legs now

4 . . . you can move your arms now

3 . . . you may want to move your head

2 . . . you can open your eyes

And 1 . . . you are fully awake

# Bibliography

1— Brown, MD, Rebecca. **He Came To Set The Captives Free**, Witaker House, Springdale, PA, 1992.

2— Chaplain, J.P. **Dictionary of Psychology, New Revised Edition**, Dell Publishing Company, Incorporated, New York, N.Y., 1975.

3— Gray, Ph.D., John. **Men Are From Mars, Women Are From Venus**, Harper Collins, New York, N.Y., 1951.

4— Hartdegen, Stephen, J. and Ceroke, Christian P., **The New American Bible**, C World Bible Publishers, Iowa Falls, Iowa, 1991.

5— Houston, John P., Bee, Helen, and Rimm, David C., **Invitation to Psychology, Second Edition**, Academic Press, Inc., New York, N.Y., 1983.

6— Lemonick, Michael D. *Glimpses of the Mind*, Time magazine, pp. 44-52, July 17, 1995.

7— Peck, M.D., M. Scott. **The Road Less Traveled**, Simon & Schuster, Rockefeller Center, 1230 Ave. of the Americas, New York, N.Y., 1978.

8— Picker, Lauren. *The Seven Pillars of Confidence*, Self magazine, pp. 157-159, May 1996.

9- United Bible Societies. **Good News Bible**, American Bible Society, New York, N.Y. 1976.

10—Williams, II, Psy.D. Earle H. **Psychology and Scripture, audio book**, Self-published, Norfolk, VA, 1990.

11— Zilbergeld, Bernie and Lazarus, Arnold A. **Mind Power**, Little, Brown and Company, Toronto, Canada, Boston, MA, 1987.

12—Rosenthal, R. and Jacobson, L., **Pygmalion in the Classroom: Teacher Expectation and Pupils' Intellectual Development**, Holt, Rinehart and Wilson, New York, N.Y., 1968.